# Southwest Foraging for Beginners

*Unveiling Nature's Hidden Treasures –*
*Your Essential Field Guide to Wild Edibles*

# Table of Contents

# Introduction

The Southwestern United States is a magical region with various terrains and wild edibles to forage. Whether an outdoor enthusiast or a curious beginner, this guide is here to make your foraging journey simple, enjoyable, and rewarding.

While you can find any foraging guide and start your journey, sticking to this book can make your foraging experience pleasant. It's made especially for you, with easy-to-understand language that breaks down complex ideas. You don't need any prior knowledge to get started. All you need is this book, a curiosity to explore, and a love for nature.

**What You'll Discover Inside**

- **Simple Instructions:** This book guides you on finding, picking, and using wild plants. Each section is filled with practical tips that are easy to follow so you can forage safely and confidently.

- **Beautiful Photos and Illustrations:** High-quality pictures and detailed images will help you identify plants quickly. If you learn through visuals, you'll find these resources incredibly helpful.

- **Respect for Nature:** Foraging isn't just about gathering plants. The most crucial aspect of foraging is caring for the environment. You will be taught how to harvest plants in a way that keeps nature healthy and thriving.

- **Traditional Uses:** Discover these plants' traditional uses and significance throughout history.

Besides providing information on foraging, this book can be your path to connecting with nature on a deeper level. You'll uncover the hidden treasures of the desert, like the sweet fruits of the prickly pear cactus and the nutritious seeds of the mesquite tree. As you explore, you'll appreciate the beauty and diversity of the Southwestern landscape.

Whether you are planning to traverse through hot deserts, climb rugged mountains, or explore expansive plateaus, this book will introduce you to every wild edible you can forage in the Southwestern region. With straightforward instructions, pictures, and a focus on ethical foraging and sustainability, this foraging guide provides all the information you need to begin your foraging journey.

Imagine walking through the desert, feeling the sun's warmth on your skin and the slipping sand beneath your feet. You spot a prickly pear cactus in the distance. With the knowledge shared in this book, you can confidently approach the plant, knowing exactly how to harvest its delicious bounty.

The book even has a chapter dedicated to making mouth-watering and delicious recipes you can try while sitting around a campfire with friends, sharing laughter as you feast on a meal made entirely from wild edibles.

The thrill of discovering new plants, the satisfaction of gathering your food, and the joy of reaping nature's bounty are what you will get after you complete this awesome foraging guidebook. Keep reading to dive into the world of wild edibles and discover their natural benefits and flavors that make the Southwest a forager's paradise.

# Chapter 1: Getting Started with Foraging in the Southwest

Whether you are a seasoned forager or just beginning to explore the natural bounty of your surroundings, this guide has information to help you discover and appreciate the unique edible treasures of the Southwest.

The Southwest region is one of the world's most diverse and intriguing foraging terrains. It includes states like Arizona, New Mexico, and parts of California and Nevada, housing a diverse range of wild edibles. These include mushrooms, cacti (prickly pear and cholla), wild greens (like purslane), nuts, berries, and more.

The Southwest region is one of the world's most diverse and intriguing foraging terrains.[1]

If you love foraging, the Southwest is the perfect region to explore. Recently, there has been a growing interest in foraging as part of the broader movements toward sustainable living, local food sourcing, and reconnecting with nature. In the Southwest, you can find workshops, guided tours, and organizations raising awareness about the edible flora of the area.

Here are the different terrains you will encounter in your foraging expeditions throughout the Southwest region.

## Deserts

The Southwest is home to some of the most iconic deserts in North America, including the Sonoran, Mojave, and Chihuahuan deserts. These hot, dry environments seem inhospitable at first glance, but they are teeming with life for those who know where to look. Edible and nutritious cacti, like the prickly pear and saguaro, are available in abundance. Furthermore, desert shrubs like creosote and mesquite provide seeds and pods that have been used for centuries by indigenous peoples. Besides these mentions, there are various wild edibles you can forage in these scorching deserts.

## Mountains

The rugged mountain ranges of the Southwestern landscape include some mentions like the Rocky Mountains, Sierra Nevada, and various smaller ranges that keep the environment cool, creating a feasible environment for many wild edibles to grow and thrive. Here, you can find an array of berries, nuts, and greens. Pine nuts from the piñon pine, wild onions, and mushrooms can be foraged in these higher elevations. The plant life here is diverse as different elevations create varied microclimates, allowing different plants to grow without a problem.

## Plateaus

The Colorado Plateau has a unique environment where high desert and forested areas intersect. This creates a diverse ecosystem where you can find a blend of desert and mountain flora. Juniper berries, wild grasses, and edible flowers are just some of the treasures that can be found on these vast plateaus. The subtle changes in altitude, climate, and geography in these areas support the growth of various plant species, each coming in a different season and with a unique method of foraging.

# Fundamental Insights for Foraging

As you begin your foraging journey in the Southwest, remember to gather as much basic knowledge as you can and respect the environment. Here are a few key principles to get you started.

### Identification Is Key

Properly identifying plants is necessary for safe and successful foraging. When you know how to identify a wild edible and information on its poisonous look-alikes, there's no chance you will be empty-handed when foraging in virtually any terrain. Take it up a notch by joining a local foraging group to learn from experienced foragers.

### Sustainable Harvesting

Remember to forage responsibly and take only what you need. Furthermore, over-foraging should be avoided, as it will only disrupt the ecosystem and even halt the growth of wild edibles. For example, if you damage the mushroom mycelium (body) and don't leave some behind, there's a high chance that these mushrooms won't grow back in the area.

### Respect the Land

Although the Southwestern terrain provides an amazing food source, it's also a cultural and spiritual home for many indigenous peoples. When foraging near settlements or areas inhabited by people, it's better to seek permission where necessary and show respect for the land and its history.

### Seasonal Awareness

Different plants are available at different times of the year. While summer and spring bring abundant foraging opportunities, it's winter when there is relatively less growth and fewer chances of foraging. Understanding the seasonal patterns of the region will help you make the most of your foraging efforts.

### Stay Safe

The arid environment of the Southwest can be harsh. Always bring sufficient water, wear appropriate clothing, and be mindful of the weather and wildlife. With each foraging expedition, you will gain a greater appreciation for the beauty of the Southwestern ecosystems. While foraging can be practiced as a contemporary hobby or a trendy lifestyle choice, this practice is deeply rooted in human history and key to the survival of countless generations.

Foraging has profound historical significance in the Southwestern United States, particularly within indigenous cultures, where it has long been the foundation of life, culture, and sustenance. Today, foraging is experiencing a resurgence as people seek more sustainable living practices and reconnect with nature and traditional knowledge in meaningful ways.

**To summarize everything you have just read, here is a rundown on how to sustainably forage a prickly pear cactus:**

### Correct Identification

Prickly pear cacti (Opuntia spp.) are easily identifiable by their flat, paddle-shaped pads and colorful fruit. It's important to distinguish them from similar-looking but inedible or protected species like the Arizona hedgehog cactus. Foraging protected species can also have serious legal consequences.

Although the prickly pear is not endangered, you must still forage sustainably. Read and learn about the plant's life cycle, its role in the local ecosystem, and any legal restrictions on foraging in the area.

### Selective Harvesting

Choose young, bright green pads (about four to eight inches long), as these are more tender and flavorful. Older pads are tougher and more fibrous. Use a sharp knife or pruning shears to cut pads from the joint where they connect to the plant, minimizing injury to the cactus.

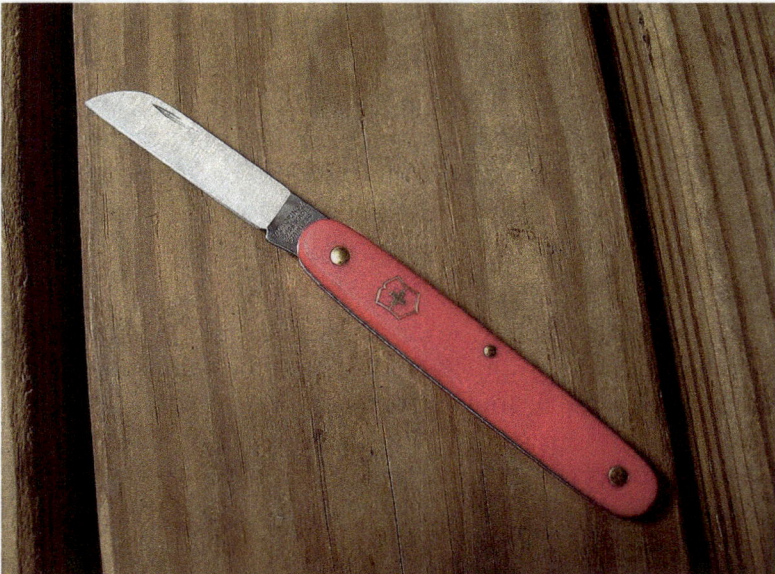

Use a sharp knife to cut pads.[3]

Harvest fruit that is deep red, purple, or yellow, indicating ripeness. The fruit should be slightly soft to the touch. Gently twist and pull or cut the fruit from the pad, being careful not to damage the pads or other fruit.

Do not tear or break pads off, as this can create larger wounds that are harder for the cactus to heal. A clean cut helps the plant heal more efficiently and reduces the risk of disease or pest infestation.

### Timing

Only harvest the pads in spring and early summer when they are actively growing and most tender. Likewise, the fruits are best harvested in late summer to early fall when they are fully ripe and nutritious.

### Spread Out Harvesting

Do not harvest all pads or fruit from a single plant or concentrated area. Instead, take a small amount from different plants spread over a wide area. This approach ensures that individual plants and the overall population remain healthy and can continue to thrive and reproduce.

### Historical Significance of Foraging

For thousands of years, the indigenous peoples of the Southwest have gathered knowledge of their environment, developing sophisticated methods for identifying, harvesting, and utilizing the region's diverse plant life. The Navajo, Apache, Hopi, and Pueblo tribes have long relied on foraging to supplement their diets, medicines, and materials for daily life. This traditional ecological knowledge is deeply woven into cultural and spiritual norms and passed on to future generations to ensure survival.

### Edible and Medicinal Plants

With trial and error, indigenous foragers became experts in identifying edible plants, like amaranth, chia, and various cacti. They understood the seasons and conditions in which these plants thrived, and they developed techniques for processing and preserving them. For example, mesquite pods were ground into flour, and prickly pear fruits were preserved. Medicinal plants like yucca and sage were also foraged and used in various traditional healing practices.

### Sustainable Practices

Sustainability was the main principle in indigenous foraging practices. Indigenous peoples practiced selective harvesting, ensuring plants could regenerate and continue providing resources. This deep respect for the land created a balanced relationship with nature, where the ecosystem's health was the focus.

## Cultural Significance

Foraging was more than a means of survival for these tribes. They used various foraged plants in ceremonies. Furthermore, gathering and preparing food often brought people together, and certain plants held significant spiritual value, which were featured prominently in rituals and traditions.

## Modern Foraging

In recent years, as people have become more aware of environmental issues and seek to reduce their ecological footprints, foraging has been an excellent way to reconnect with nature and promote sustainability.

Most modern foragers contribute to environmental conservation by relying less on industrial agriculture, which is seen as the root cause of habitat disturbances, pollution, and high carbon emissions. Foraging encourages the protection of wild spaces and biodiversity, as keeping these ecosystems thriving enables wild edibles to grow and be available for foraging.

## Community and Education

People's increasing interest in foraging has also promoted community building and education. Foraging groups and workshops are becoming more common, where people share knowledge, experiences, and techniques. Besides its environmental benefits, foraging has significant personal health and well-being advantages. It encourages physical activity and a deeper appreciation for nature. For many, foraging becomes a meditative practice, providing a break from the fast-paced, technology-driven modern world.

Despite the dryness and harsh conditions of the Southwest, this terrain holds a surprisingly bountiful array of wild edibles for those with the knowledge and skills to forage.

## The Arid Nature of the Southwest

The Southwest's environment has scorching summers, minimal rainfall, and vast stretches of arid terrain. Yet, precisely, these challenging conditions have promoted a unique and diverse array of plant life, each species finely adapted to survive and thrive. The deserts of the Southwest, like the Sonoran, Mojave, and Chihuahuan, along with its high-altitude plateaus and mountainous regions, create a mosaic of microhabitats, each with unique edible plants.

Mojave desert.[*]

## Potential for a Bountiful Harvest

The Southwest can provide surprisingly plentiful harvests for those who know where and how to look. Here are a few examples of the types of wild edibles you might find:

- **Prickly Pear Cactus (Opuntia, spp. – which means "multiple species"):** This cactus is recognizable by its flat, paddle-shaped edible pads (nopales) and vibrant fruits (tunas), which are abundant in vitamins and minerals.

- **Mesquite (Prosopis spp.):** Mesquite trees have sweet, protein-rich pods that can be ground into flour, which can be used for baking.

- **Yucca (Yucca spp.):** The yucca plant's flowers, stalks, and fruits are edible, and its roots have been traditionally used for their medicinal properties.

- **Piñon Pine (Pinus edulis):** Piñon pines produce delicious pine nuts, a highly nutritious food that has been harvested by indigenous peoples for centuries.

- **Agave (Agave spp.):** Agave plants yield sweet sap (aguamiel) and fibrous leaves that can be roasted or fermented to produce a variety of foods and beverages.

- **Wild Amaranth (Amaranthus spp.):** The leaves and seeds of wild amaranth are edible and offer a valuable source of nutrition with high protein and mineral content.
- **Cholla Cactus (Cylindropuntia spp.):** The buds of this cactus can be harvested and prepared for consumption.
- **Purslane (Portulaca oleracea):** This is a succulent plant found in disturbed soils. Its leaves are full of omega-3 fatty acids and can be eaten raw or cooked.
- **Desert Sage (Salvia dorrii):** Known for its aromatic leaves, it can be used as a seasoning or in teas.
- **Wild Onions (Allium spp.):** These are found in various habitats and add a delicious, pungent flavor to dishes.

These examples are a handful of the potential bounty the Southwest's arid landscape can provide. With the right knowledge and respect for the environment, you can uncover a wealth of edibles hidden within this rugged and resilient region.

# Practical Tips for Novices

While foraging is a rewarding and enriching experience, it requires a solid foundation of knowledge and skills, particularly in plant identification. As a novice, developing this expertise is crucial for your safety and the sustainability of your foraging activities. Here are some practical tips to help you get started, emphasizing the basic concepts of plant identification and the necessity of using multiple resources to practice safe foraging.

Although it will take time, start by learning the different plant names and their parts.

- Observe the shape, size, arrangement (opposite, alternate, or whorled), edge (smooth, serrated, lobed), and vein pattern.
- Note the color, texture, and distinguishing features like thorns or hair.
- Look at the number of petals, color, shape, and arrangement.
- If it's a fruit, identify the type (berries, nuts, pods), color, shape of the seeds, and size.

### Use a Systematic Approach

Besides learning about plant identification, you must gather more information on their habitat, the season they can forage, and their growth patterns.

- Note where the plant is growing. For example, desert plants have different adaptations than those in mountainous areas.
- Recognize that different plants appear at different times of the year. Keep track of what you see and when you see it.
- Look at how the plant grows and note its visual appearance. For example, wild berries grow on vines, whereas mesquite pods grow on trees.

### Identifying Poisonous Look-Alikes

Learn to distinguish between similar-looking plants by noting subtle differences. This is crucial to avoid consuming toxic look-alikes.

- You must not rely on one source for plant identification.
- In addition to using the information in this foraging guide, you must take additional steps to verify the plant's identity before foraging.
- Utilizing online plant databases and related apps to cross-check your findings is the best approach.

### Start with Easy-to-Identify Plants

Although you can read about all the wild plants found in the Southwest in one go, it's better to start with the easily recognizable edibles. For example, a prickly pear cactus has distinct pads and fruits. Likewise, piñon pine trees produce pine nuts.

### Join Foraging Groups or Take Classes

Take your learning up a notch by joining local foraging groups for hands-on learning and foraging trips where you can practice what you have learned. Many areas in the region also provide guided foraging walks and workshops, which can be invaluable if you have just started foraging.

### Practice Safe Foraging

Take only what you need and leave enough for the wild edible to reproduce and for wildlife to feed on. Ensure the plants you forage are not rare, restricted, or endangered in your area. Furthermore, avoid foraging near roadsides, industrial areas, or places where pesticides are used.

When trying a new plant, consume a small amount first to check for any adverse reactions. You also have to make sure foraging is allowed in the area you're exploring. Some public lands require permits, and private land requires permission from the owner.

### Sustainable Harvesting Practices

While you can forage it all, make it a habit to harvest small amounts of any given plant to ensure there is enough left to sustain the plant population and the wildlife that relies on it. For example, iguanas, coyotes, jackrabbits, and various other animals survive by eating the prickly pear cactus in the desert.

Animals survive by eating the prickly pear cactus in the desert, so take what you need and leave the rest for wildlife.'

The general rule of thumb is never to exceed foraging more than one-third of a plant or plant population to allow for regrowth and reproduction. Furthermore, keep rotating your foraging locations to prevent local overharvesting and allow the plant populations to recover.

You must read about how and when the plants you forage reproduce. For example, some plants are annuals that need to set seed each year, while perennials might have different harvesting times. Knowing their reproductive cycles makes it easier to pinpoint a timeframe where you can harvest the plant species.

### Respect for the Environment

Be mindful of where you step to avoid trampling on plants and disturbing habitats. Stick to established trails whenever possible to avoid trampling on plants or insects in the environment.

Whatever you bring in, including any litter, must be brought back with you. Avoid leaving any signs of your presence in the foraging area.

### Avoid Contaminated Areas

Avoid foraging in areas that may be contaminated by pesticides, herbicides, heavy metals, or other pollutants, like roadsides, industrial sites, and agricultural fields. Be cautious when foraging near water sources. Ensure the water is clean and free of pollutants to prevent contaminating the plants you harvest.

### Protect Endangered and Sensitive Species

Familiarize yourself with local, state, and federal laws regarding protected species and foraging regulations. Some plants are protected by law due to their endangered status. Use local foraging resources like extension services and conservation organizations to learn more about endangered and sensitive species in the area you plan to forage.

### Promote Plant Growth

If you love to connect with nature, you can use foraging to support the environment further. You can help propagate plants by spreading seeds in suitable habitats when appropriate. For example, in the Southwest, March is the most suitable time to propagate seeds. This can include planting native species, removing invasive species, and supporting pollinator habitats.

This support for the environment can replenish plant populations and support biodiversity. However, you might need to join plant conservation organizations to learn the processes used to promote plant growth.

You can also use proper pruning techniques to encourage healthy regrowth of plants.

### Cultural and Ethical Sensitivity

Although many areas with native populations have turned into urban areas in the Southwest, various tribes, like the Apache tribe, live in Arizona and the Navajo. When foraging on lands traditionally owned or managed by Indigenous communities, seek permission and follow any guidelines they provide.

### Community Respect

Before you start foraging in a private area or property, seek permission and respect the rights and wishes of the landowners. If it's public land, adhere to regulations and guidelines set by public land management agencies. This includes national parks, forests, and other public lands where foraging might be restricted or regulated.

Foraging is much more than picking wild foods or just finding your next meal in the wild. It is a deeply personal journey into nature that demands you to form a sustainable relationship with the environment. To forage ethically, you need to think about how your actions affect the ecosystems you're exploring. This means harvesting in a way that allows plants to regenerate, minimizing your impact on the surroundings, protecting species at risk, and respecting the cultural significance these practices hold for local communities.

Adopting these principles ensures that nature's bounty remains available for future explorers and deepens your connection with the land. As you step into foraging, especially in the Southwest's unique terrains, you're following in the footsteps of countless generations before you. These regions with expansive arid lands house edible plants that have sustained indigenous peoples for thousands of years. Your journey here is not just about gathering food but about understanding and preserving these traditions and the land itself.

In the chapters to come, you'll dig deeper into this rich and rewarding world of wild edibles. You'll learn to identify plants, read about their seasons and habitats, and discover how to harvest them sustainably and respectfully. You will explore practical tips and detailed descriptions that will set you up to forage confidently and ethically.

Get ready to explore the delicious bounty that awaits you in the Southwest. From the sweet fruits of the prickly pear cactus to the nutritious seeds of the mesquite tree, you'll uncover the nutritious treasures of this unique region. You'll soon discover that foraging is a skill that opens up a new way of seeing the world around you. Each plant becomes a potential source of nourishment, and each foraging trip will teach you something new and helpful. You'll learn to identify various plants, understand their seasons and habitats, and learn how to harvest them without causing harm. With the right information in hand and a mindful approach, you're set to unlock the sustainable foods of the Southwest. Seize this chance to nourish yourself and develop a connection with the natural world.

# Chapter 2: Essential Foraging Equipment, Tools, and Safety

During the Paleolithic Era (Old Stone Age), humans mostly hunted wild animals for food. However, when wildlife was scarce, they feasted on wild edibles. Since they barely had any tools, they may have been pulling the edible plants from the roots with their hands, never knowing the damage they caused to the environment until much later.

Use the necessary tools to cut the plant just above the root so you don't cause damage to the land.[5]

Back in the day, people didn't have the knowledge or the equipment for sustainable foraging. Did you know that if you pull plants along with their roots, the land will eventually become infertile? You should cut the plant above the root, for which you will need tools like scissors or knives. The right tools and equipment not only ensure your safety but also the environment.

## The Importance of Proper Preparation

It is entirely possible to forage for wild edibles with just you and your hands. You can hold the plant at the base and pluck a branch or simply forage for fruits, flowers, and berries. However, it is also possible to accidentally pluck the roots this way, which may cause irreparable damage to the soil.

When you pull the roots along with the plant, you rob the microorganisms in the soil of their main food source. They will either migrate to other parts of the land or die. What's wrong with losing a few microbes? There are plenty in the world, after all.

The relationship between microbes and roots isn't one way but a give-and-take mechanism. Those microscopic creatures help cycle nutrients back to the roots, promoting further plant growth. They also break down the roots into fundamental components to create new plants.

Thus, if you want to find more plants for foraging in the area after your first session, you will need to maintain the population of microbes, which can only be done if you don't pull out the roots of edible plants. The only surefire way of doing this is by using tools like knives or scissors.

Additionally, what if thorny plants like cacti or poisonous plants can prick you while plucking to transfer their poison? Most regions of the Southwest are defined by extreme heat. Dangerous wild creatures like bears and snakes are also prominent in the region.

Your safety is as important as the environment's, and the right tools will protect you both. Other factors to consider are:

- Some wild foods may grow in hard-to-reach or densely vegetated areas. You can't hope to walk around in the scorching sun without a stick or pole for support. You may also need to traverse a prickly part of the terrain to reach edible plants in the forest.

- While most edibles can be identified with the naked eye, what if a certain plant's characteristics are so tiny that you cannot see them without a magnifier? You may end up consuming a poisonous plant.

- Protection from the elements is paramount in the wild. Animal threats can be detected from afar, but what about extreme heat or an impending storm?

- Many of the most bountiful foraging regions in the Southwest are far from civilization. As you dive deeper into the heart of the wild, you may not know which way you came from or where you are headed. Navigation tools are critical for your survival while foraging.

- Foraging tools can serve educational purposes by facilitating hands-on learning experiences. For example, children's foraging kits containing child-friendly tools and resources encourage curiosity, exploration, and appreciation for nature.

**Understanding and Preparing for Varied Terrain**

The Southwest is known for its high temperatures, which can even rise to a sweltering 120°F. However, did you know that temperatures in regions in Utah and Arizona can go as low as -40°F in winter, which is lower than in many northern areas? These extreme temperatures can lead to heatstroke, dehydration, or hypothermia if you go guns blazing for foraging without the right tools.

Heatstroke is a medical emergency that occurs when your body temperature goes beyond 104°F due to prolonged exposure to high temperatures. Every material object in the universe tries to achieve equilibrium (a heat balance), and your body is no different.

Your average body temperature is 98.6°F. The heat exchange process begins when you spend a long time in a high-temperature environment for foraging, like the Southwest semi-arid regions of New Mexico. The environment transfers its high heat to your body (low heat) until it eventually reaches an equilibrium. Suppose you are foraging in an area with a temperature of 112°F. In that case, your body will eventually heat up to 105°F, leading to a heatstroke.

Dehydration is a common phenomenon that occurs after drinking alcohol. Its direct result is a hangover, but the direct result of foraging in a high-temperature environment can be more than just that. It can lead to urinary infections and kidney failure, which can prove to be fatal.

Hypothermia is the exact opposite of heatstroke and dehydration. When you spend time in a cold environment, like foraging near the White Mountains of Arizona (where the temperature can fall to -40°F), heat is transferred from your body to the environment, causing your body temperature to fall. The extreme effects of hypothermia are unconsciousness and memory loss.

Other types of terrain and weather that you will encounter in the Southwest are:

- In many parts of the Southwest, especially Texas, Colorado, and Oklahoma, unpredictable heavy rainfall is highly possible. It can lead to flash floods in desert canyons and washes. You need to prepare yourself for both of these eventualities.

- These regions have vast swaths of rough, treacherous terrain. You need to especially watch out for rocky canyons, steep cliffs, and cactus-strewn desert floors found in almost every southwestern state. These areas have high risks of falling, sprains, and other injuries.

- When you think about the wildlife in the Southwest, the first creature that comes to mind is the scorpion. Its sting can be fatal to humans and particularly dangerous for children and the elderly. There are also many venomous rattlesnakes and spiders in the region that you need to protect yourself from.

- Animals aren't the only venomous creatures in the area. You may come across many poisonous plants, too. Watch out for the following four:

1. **Poison Ivy:** A seemingly harmless plant can cause rashes or irritation when touched. It grows as a bush or a low shrub, with three leaves on each branch. It is usually green in color but can turn red in the fall. It is found in almost every southwestern state except parts of California.

Poison ivy. [6]

2. **Jimsonweed (Datura stramonium):** Unlike Poison Ivy, Jimsonweed is easily recognizable with its green leaves shaped like irregular waves. It's an invasive bush that produces white or violet flowers in summer, usually found in Texas. If you eat any of its parts, you will experience prolonged delirium that may be fatal.

Jimsonweed. [7]

3. **Water Hemlock (Cicuta):** This is another easily recognizable plant that is among the most poisonous plants in the world. You can identify it by its tiny white or greenish flowers that cluster together to form an umbrella shape. Its leaves are long and green with sharp edges. It can be confused with many edible plants like carrots and parsnips. Its common variant, Cicuta douglasii, is found throughout the Southwest.

Water hemlock.[8]

4. **Death Camas (Toxicoscordion Venenosum):** As the name suggests, the Death Camas is a highly toxic plant that kills anyone who eats it. Only one creature is known to endure its poison – the Death Camas miner bee. It helps spread the plant by collecting pollen for its young ones. The Death Cama's seeds and bulbous roots are its most toxic parts. Its flowers are like six-pointed stars, and the plant can grow up to 20 inches long.

Death camas. [9]

- Most of the Southwest is desert where wild edibles are moderately available, but civilization is scarce. If a scorpion stings you or you suffer from heatstroke, you may need to walk for several miles before finding medical aid. Additionally, you may wander into remote areas in search of edibles – places where there is nothing as far as the eye can see. Prepare yourself for this limited accessibility in the foraging areas of the Southwest.

# Essential Foraging Tools

The aforementioned dangers of foraging aren't to frighten you away from your hobby but to ensure that you stay safe during the adventure.

Given the sheer amount of preparations and safety precautions, you may imagine carrying several bags on your foraging trip. However, you don't want to tire yourself out too soon. Foraging is long and hard work. You need to find the right area nearby, locate edible plants, fruits, and flowers, ensure they aren't poisonous, and then collect and carry them back home.

Hence, carrying only a few vital tools and equipment is necessary – things you can keep in your pockets or a small rucksack.

- **Sturdy Basket or Bag:** You can hold the foraged goods in your hands or keep them in your pockets, especially if you are making a quick trip to a nearby park or just foraging in your backyard. However, suppose you are headed to far-off canyons, deserts, or forests. In that case, you will want to collect more than just a handful of edibles. That is when a sturdy basket or bag comes in handy.

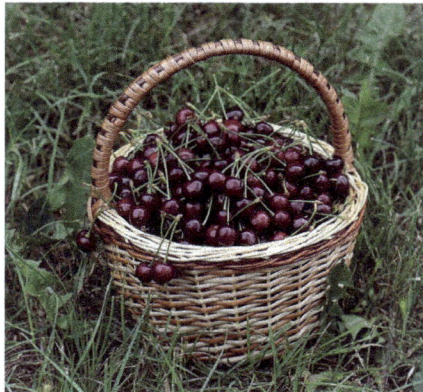

Foraging basket.[10]

Opt for something breathable to prevent trapped moisture and avoid spoilage of your goods. A flat-bottomed wicker basket is best for collecting plants. You can go with a lightweight mesh bag with a drawstring for fruits and mushrooms. If you like to fish, you can use your breathable fishing creel for foraging edibles.

- **Quality Knife or Shears:** To avoid making the land infertile, you need to ensure you don't pluck the plant from its roots unless, of course, you are foraging for edible roots like sweet potatoes. Use a quality knife for cutting stems, branches, and roots. A foldable knife can easily fit in your pocket.

Use sheers to cut thick stems. [11]

Shears are more efficient than knives, as you can quickly cut thick stems, branches, and roots. Durable foraging shears are large and heavy but can easily fit in your bag. Look for a pair with a locking mechanism so its sharp edges don't accidentally tear through your sack. You can carry scissors to cut thin plants.

Roots can sometimes be hard to pull out with your hands. A trowel will be useful if you are specifically foraging for roots and tubers. Simply dig out the soil surrounding the plant with your trowel to reach the root.

- **Reliable Field Guide:** A reliable field guide, like this book, will help you identify all edible plants, mushrooms, fruits, berries, and other forgeable items in your area. It will also help you identify any poisonous plants to avoid.

Are you collecting the right edibles in the right season? Do you want to refer to tips for sustainable foraging? A reliable field guide is an all-inclusive educational resource you can quickly check during your venture. If it's a pocketbook or a downloadable eBook, it's even better.

- **Water Bottle and Snacks:** To avoid dehydration in the scorching heat of the Southwest, c a couple of standard 16.9-ounce water bottles. Place them inside your backpack, not in the mesh containers to the sides. This will keep them away from direct sunlight, and you can use the mesh containers to store your additional edibles.

Did you know you need to eat every three to four hours to stay healthy? Eating every three to four hours helps maintain your blood sugar levels and is the ideal time for ensuring proper digestion. Have a full meal before heading out foraging, and carry a few healthy snacks if you're planning to spend more than three hours out there.

- **First-Aid Kit:** The wild is highly unpredictable. You may be more prone to accidents out there than in your city. Regardless of all your precautions, a rattlesnake can bite you, a scorpion can sting you, or you may tumble down a steep incline. The elements can also change without warning, drenching you in flash floods or covering you in snow.

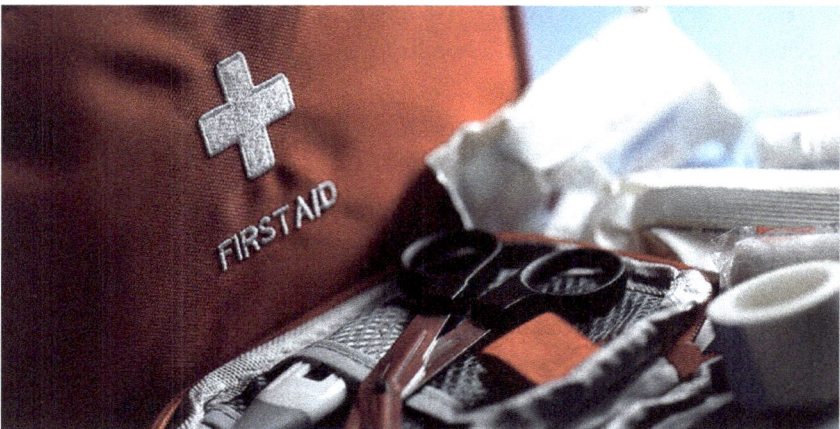

Have a first-aid kit with you when foraging. [18]

Ideally, your first-aid kit should include bandages and antibacterial wipes for wounds, antihistamine for poisonous stings and irritation, over-the-counter pain medications, blister pads for sore feet, burn gel for sunburns, and hydrocortisone cream for treating venom-based skin conditions.

- **Appropriate Clothing:** Your clothes should be lightweight and breathable, ideally made of cotton to keep you cool in hot temperatures. You may be tempted to wear shorts and sleeveless tees in the extreme heat. However, they make you more vulnerable to cuts, bites, and scratches from thorny plants and insects. Wear long-sleeved shirts and pants instead.

Sturdy hiking boots are recommended. They will provide excellent traction in rocky terrain and protect your feet from thorny plants or venomous shrubs. If you prefer something lighter and more comfortable, consider wearing trail runners. Ensure they are waterproof since you may need to cross streams or walk in the rain. You can also wear socks to keep your feet dry and prevent blisters.

- **Protective Gear:** You will need protection from the region's elements and wildlife. Buy clothes with an Ultraviolet Protection Factor (UPF) for added sun protection. Wear a hat and sunglasses to avoid headaches and heat strokes. If you plan to spend the night in an elevated region, pack protective jackets or windbreakers in your bag.

The southern parts of Arizona and New Mexico often receive heavy rainfall. Tie a rain jacket around your waist, just in case. Don textured leather gloves to protect yourself from accidental pricks and insect bites while foraging. Take an insect repelling cream or spray along for added protection.

## Additional Tools and Equipment

The tools mentioned in the previous section are absolute must-haves, especially if you are foraging for the first time. Additional tools you can consider packing are:

- **Navigational Equipment:** These will be useful if you visit unknown or unexplored terrain. It is easy to get lost in the vast desert regions and dense forests of the Southwest. Your phone may have GPS navigation, but if there's a poor connection, the maps won't load. Download the map of the region beforehand for offline viewing. There's usually an option for offline viewing in the "Settings" tab of both Android and iOS.

If technology fails, you can tell the direction from the position of the sun, moon, and other stars, but it always helps to carry a compass. Keep a paper map or an atlas of the region.

- **Magnifying Glass:** The identifying characteristics (leaf veins, flower shapes, etc.) of certain edibles aren't visible to the naked eye, as you will learn in Chapter 4. Carry a magnifying glass to classify such plants correctly.

- **Multipurpose Stick:** Take a walking stick or any stick (a straight tree branch as long as your height) with you. It will help you test the depth of a pool of water, navigate uneven terrain, and easily move shrubs and plants aside to find edible food.

# Tips to Maintain and Care for Your Tools and Equipment

Any tool or equipment doesn't stay the same way forever. The sharp edges of knives and shears can become dull or corrode, backpack straps and harnesses can wear out, foraging baskets may develop holes and tears, and the contents of your first-aid kit will expire someday. You don't want to end up in a situation where you can neither cut edible plants nor dress your wounds. Your entire trip will be a waste of time and may result in serious health problems in the future.

- **Clean After Each Use:** After each foraging trip, rinse your tools off with water and a mild detergent to remove dirt, sap, or debris. Focus on crevices and moving parts where dirt is most stubborn.

- **Dry Thoroughly:** Ensure your tools are completely dry before storing them to prevent rust and corrosion. Use a towel to wipe off excess water and keep them out to dry in the sun.

- **Sharpen Blades:** Keep your knives, shears, and other bladed tools sharp for optimal performance. Use a sharpening stone, honing rod, or sharpening tool specifically designed for your blade type.

- **Oil Moving Parts:** Lubricate hinges, pivot points, and other moving parts of your tools with a light coat of oil or lubricant to prevent rust and keep them working smoothly. You will need to switch up the lubricant depending on the material of your tools. For instance, mineral oil is ideal for wooden handles, and silicone spray is used for metal parts.

- **Store Properly:** Store your foraging tools in a clean and dry environment away from moisture, direct sunlight, and extreme temperatures. Hang them on hooks or store them in a dedicated toolbox to prevent damage.

- **Protect Blades:** Wear blade guards or sheaths to protect the sharp edges of knives and other bladed tools while carrying them in your backpack. This prevents accidental cuts and maintains the blade's sharpness.

- **Replace Worn Parts and Expired Medicines:** Knife handles usually need replacing after multiple heavy uses. The blades will also lose their strength after being sharpened multiple times. Buy brand-new shears and knives or replace the worn-out parts. Additionally, don't forget to replace expired medicines. They may prove to be ineffective or have harmful side effects after consumption.

Did you know over 6,000 foragers in the U.S. suffer from accidental poisoning each year? This is mainly because they lack the required safety gear or the knowledge to effectively steer away from the dangers of the activity. Remember that a well-prepared forager is observant and considers the well-being of themselves and the environment.

Carrying all the necessities with you isn't much of a task. Think about it: the combined weight of the key tools won't be more than five pounds, and you can easily carry it all in an eight-gallon backpack. Coupled with your lightweight clothing appropriate for the weather and the terrain, you can stroll right into the heart of nature as if you're carrying nothing at all.

You can indulge in your foraging activity without worrying about venomous bites, pricks, unforeseen accidents, or rough weather. You are already prepared for the worst; it's time to enjoy the best parts of the natural world that await.

# Chapter 3: Seasonal Foraging in the Southwest

You may wonder if plant life and other edibles are scarce in the Southwest. After all, much of it is dry, desert land and rocky terrain. In summer, the temperature often goes beyond your body temperature, which begs the question: are edibles rarely found in the extreme heat? Do experienced foragers stock up for summer like the people beyond the Arctic Circle do for winter?

There are plenty of edibles to forage all year round.[18]

*Not at all!*

Many edible plants and fruits have adapted to thrive in the deserts' extreme heat or the mountain peaks' unnatural cold. There are plenty of edibles to forage all year round, be it in the cheerful spring climate or during the colorful fall season. Only the types of edibles will differ depending on the season.

# Spring Season

While the spring season is often unpredictable in the Southwest, it usually starts earlier than the rest of the U.S. (from March to June). It's a time when the arid desert environment undergoes a miraculous transformation to lush greenery and beautiful flowers of almost every color on the spectrum.

Fields of wildflowers blanket the desert floor, their delicate petals swaying in the breeze like a sea of living paint strokes. Brilliant shades of yellow, orange, purple, and pink carpet the ground, transforming the once-barren terrain into a botanical wonderland. Ripe foraging edibles are nestled amid these visual marvels, ready for the taking.

The temperature drops to a pleasant 50°F, so you won't need to wear any special or additional clothing. Carry your foraging bag and a few tools, and go explore the countryside for the many delicacies that have sprouted.

### The Terrain

Spring is an ideal time to explore the iconic beauty of the region while foraging. The weather is mild, even in the afternoon, so you can take a day trip to a nearby canyon or desert to search for food. There's the Grand Canyon in Arizona, Bryce Canyon in Utah, and Canyonlands National Park.

Arizona's Sonoran Desert, California's Anza-Borrego Desert, and parts of Nevada and New Mexico burst into bloom with a variety of desert wildflowers like brittlebush, desert marigold, lupine, and cacti. Admire the stark contrast of these vivid colors against the dreary desert terrain as you forage the area.

There's no heavy rainfall in the spring, but occasionally, you may experience light showers. Don't run for cover; take in the beauty of the region augmented by the rains as the skies darken, but the land remains colorful. If you are in the desert, the enchanting smell of wet earth will take you on another plane.

The gentle patter of rain on the desert floor and the rhythmic dripping from the foliage create a soothing backdrop. Additionally, it often brings out a chorus of wildlife. Frogs emerge from their hiding spots to croak all day long, and birds sing with renewed vigor, their calls echoing across the drenched canyons and wide valleys.

In the mountains of Arizona, New Mexico, Colorado, and Utah, spring writes a different but no less enchanting story. As the snow melts and mountain meadows come to life with wildflowers, ponderosa pine forests and aspen groves awaken from their winter slumber, creating picturesque scenes of greenery against snow-capped peaks.

Rivers and waterfalls start flowing freely, fed by melting snow and spring rains. Places like Havasu Falls in the Grand Canyon, Zion National Park in Utah, and the waterfalls of the Sierra Nevada Mountains offer stunning displays of cascading water against the backdrop of rugged terrains. Indeed, spring is the perfect time for foraging while admiring nature's beauty.

### Availability of Plants

You will find plenty of foraging opportunities when you step out of the city and into any natural environment. Spring is the time when you can comfortably pick and choose your favorite edibles. However, the availability of plants depends on the type of terrain you are scouring.

The prickly pear cactus pads and fruit are delicious. You can find them in any desert region throughout the Southwest. Look for mesquite pods and agave stalks, too, while you're at it. Chia seeds can be found on desert slopes, and Yucca fruits and flowers can be collected from the rocky parts of the area. Forage in low desert areas like the Sonoran and Mojave deserts for better prospects.

If there is a mountain range nearby, you can collect pinyon pines and mesquite pods since they are usually found at higher elevations. Visit the New Mexico mountains or the Arizona uplands. The Southwest doesn't have a coastline, but a part of Southern California does. You can find chia seeds and wild mustard there.

Don't forget to keep an eye out on the roadsides, gardens, or open fields for hidden gems while you are traveling to your foraging location. There's a high possibility of finding plants like amaranth, lamb's quarters, and purslane.

## Quick Tips and Precautions

- Spring is a time of growth and renewal, so look for young shoots, fresh greens, and blossoming plants. Many desert plants will produce new growth after winter rains.

- Learn to identify the local flora, focusing on plants that are at their peak in spring, such as wild mustard, miner's lettuce, and mesquite pods.

- The best time to forage is when plants are well-hydrated and fresh after rainfall.

- Springtime is a feasting time for animals, too. Take only what you need and leave enough for your fellow living beings. For instance, pinyon pine nuts are the preferred food source for most wildlife and Indigenous peoples in the Southwest.

- Be wary of snakes and other dangerous wildlife emerging from hibernation during this time.

- To avoid accidental bites, don't collect fruits and flowers with bees or ants on them. Especially watch out for spiders hiding in low shrubs or on tree branches.

# Summer Season

The dreaded Southwest summer isn't as dreadful as it's often portrayed. It can even be pleasant at times, especially for foraging. Imagine stepping into the heart of the desert, where the air is thick with the scent of sage, mingling with the faint aroma of distant rain. It's a harsh, rugged terrain, but the sky above is a brilliant blue interrupted only by the occasional wisp of a cloud.

The sun beats down with unrelenting intensity, yet colorful wildflowers, bountiful fruits, and thorny cacti thrive, their arms reaching toward the heavens as if challenging the extreme heat in a silent prayer for rain. The distant call of a coyote echoes across the canyon, lizards bask on the rocky landscape, and a solitary hawk circles up high.

The summer temperature in the Southwest is usually in excess of 100°F, so you need to wear light cotton clothes and carry at least half a gallon of water. Foraging opportunities are plenty, but you may have to walk long distances to find the right edibles.

## The Terrain

If you are a beginner in the foraging world, it is recommended not to venture into deserts or canyons in the summer without proper preparation. The land won't be completely barren, but there may not be anyone for miles around in case you run out of water or find it difficult to handle the intense heat.

Start by foraging in parks or forests in and around your neighborhood. Get used to the relatively mild heat of civilization before venturing into the scorching parts of the Southwest. In the deserts, you will find rolling sand dunes, rocky hills, and vast expanses of scrubland. Vegetation will usually be scattered across large areas of barren sand.

Start with a mild region like the Chihuahuan Desert in Texas. [14]

The Sonoran desert in the southernmost part of the U.S. and the Mojave desert in California are the hottest deserts in the region. Start with a milder region like the Chihuahuan Desert in Texas, where the temperature rarely exceeds 90°F.

The Colorado Plateau is a vast expanse of occasional jutting rock formations, but it isn't entirely devoid of vegetation. Forage on higher elevations where the temperature is around 70°F. Canyons have extremely high temperatures in the daytime, especially in the deep gorges. Visit at dawn or just after dusk to experience a cooler atmosphere.

Mountains are the best places to forage in the summer. If you climb high enough, you will experience a cool 60°F environment even in the afternoon. The Rocky Mountains of New Mexico, Colorado, Utah, and the Sierra Nevada range in California are perfect foraging spots at any time of the day or night.

### Availability of Plants

Almost all the edibles found in the spring season come to full bloom in the summer. Between June and September, you will get to forage the most delicious parts of spring edibles. The fruits of the prickly pear cactus turn an attractive pink in the extreme heat, particularly during mid to late summer. They are full of vitamins and antioxidants, helping you reduce weight and improve skin health. Your long trip to the closest desert will be well worth it.

Mesquite pods turn golden and brittle in the summer. You can dry and grind them into a sweet flour high in protein and fiber but low in fat. The cones of pinyon pine nuts open late in the summer, but they won't last for long. They are hot favorites among many animals in the Southwest, so it will be a race between you and the wildlife.

**A Pro Tip:** Start foraging in the mountains or woodlands nearby from August to find fresh pine nuts.

In the early summer, when the sun isn't very intense, you can forage for the flower buds of the cholla cactus, leaves and stems of the amaranth, leaves of lamb's quarters, flowers of wild mustard, and agave stalks. The edibles are even more rewarding late in the season, with agave plants offering sweet nectar that can be harvested for use in cooking or as a natural sweetener. The seeds of mustard, lamb's quarters, and amaranth are matured enough to be collected. The fruits of the cholla cactus also become ripe enough to eat.

### Quick Tips and Precautions

- Avoid foraging when the sun is at its zenith. Early morning at around 8:00 AM and late afternoon (around 5:00 PM) are perfect times for the activity.

- Wait for the occasional summer rainfall. The desert comes alive after rain, making plants more vibrant and easier to spot.

- Carry plenty of water – more than you think you'll need. Dehydration and heat exhaustion are serious risks in the desert during summer.

- Take frequent breaks in shaded areas to avoid overexertion. Carry a lightweight tarp or shade cloth if the natural shade is sparse.

- Watch out for snakes, spiders, and scorpions. They are more active throughout the summertime.

- Wear a wide-brimmed hat, sunglasses, and sunscreen. Lightweight, long-sleeved shirts and pants can also protect your skin from the sun and thorns.

# Fall Season

As the oppressive heat of summer begins to wane, it makes way for more temperate days and cool, crisp nights. The region, known for its arid deserts, towering mountains, and expansive plateaus, becomes a canvas painted with the hues of autumn. The cooler weather rejuvenates both the land and its inhabitants, offering a welcome reprieve from the summer's intensity and a prelude to the cold of winter.

The desert temperatures start dipping in the evening, with average lows of around 50°F. Plateaus and canyons become even cooler, with minimum temperatures going below the 30-degree mark. The trees and shrubs mimic the color of the land – a bright orange-yellow hue. Due to this natural camouflage, you may find it difficult to locate edibles unless you have mastered the identification techniques discussed in the following chapter.

Plants enter a period of dormancy, but there are many good enough to eat. Desert plants bloom a second time, and the forests are a sight to behold with their red, orange, and yellow colors.

## The Terrain

The temperature is bearable during the fall, and the arid environment is inviting. This season, many of the classic pictures of saguaros standing tall amid a sea of shrubs are taken. Creosote bushes, ocotillo, and mesquite trees add to the desert's resilient flora. Occasional bursts of red and yellow appear from the foliage of these plants preparing for winter.

The plateaus feature stunning red rock formations, deep canyons, and expansive mesas. Due to their slightly higher position, the atmosphere can become chilly at night. In the Grand Canyon, the hiking season has just begun. Towering golden trees adorn the Colorado River, and the canyon's sheer cliffs and deep gorges are particularly breathtaking.

The mountain ranges in the region look as if they have emerged straight out of an oil painting. You can find almost every shade of green, yellow, and red imaginable against a mesmerizing backdrop of snow-capped peaks.

In essence, the fall terrain of the Southwest is a captivating blend of rugged beauty and kaleidoscopic colors. From semi-arid deserts and towering mountain ranges to colorful plateaus and faintly blooming canyons, it's a visual feast of autumnal hues and textures. Cooler temperatures and clear skies make it an ideal time for foraging and exploring the vast countryside.

## Availability of Plants

Spring may be the best time for foraging, but the fall isn't too far behind. The fruits and flowers that have already ripened and bloomed in late summer retain their freshness throughout the fall season. So, you will find fully ripe fruits of the prickly pear cactus, the cholla cactus, the hackberry, and wild grapes.

You can find wild grapes even in the fall. [15]

If you thought the mesquite pods on trees were abundant in the summer, behold them in the fall. It will look like the entire tree is covered in pods rather than leaves! You can grind them into flour or brew them into a sweet, nutty coffee. Walnuts are unique to this season (available late in the fall) and are usually found along streams and riverbanks. Collect them once they fall to the ground and remove the husks before eating.

Unless the wildlife in the mountainous regions has eaten them all, pinyon pine nuts will be available throughout the season. Collect fallen acorns late in the season. You can shell them and leach out the tannins by soaking them in water before eating. Then there are wild persimmons, which may be a bit difficult to find. They usually ripen in September, but the trees are few and far between in the Southwest.

### Quick Tips and Precautions

- In addition to the basic foraging tools, carry tongs to pluck the prickly pear fruits because, like the plant, they have spines.
- The specialty of prickly pear pads in the fall season is their tenderness and wholesome flavor. You won't find pads that taste as good in any other season.
- Most of the fruits are sweet and can be eaten raw or made into jellies.
- Don't grind your mesquite pods right after bringing them home. Let them dry completely.
- Anything you aren't eating right away should be dried and stored to extend its shelf life.
- The fall weather in the Southwest is often unpredictable. One moment, the skies may be clear, but the next, there could be heavy rainfall that will cause flash floods, especially in arid regions.

# Winter Season

The Southwest winter isn't as cold as the other parts of the U.S. The Alaskan residents would call it summer! Many parts of the Southwest receive moderate snowfall, and many others experience none. It's usually a season of serene beauty and striking contrasts instead of purely white terrain.

From the sun-soaked deserts and their resilient flora to the snow-dusted plateaus and majestic, snow-covered mountains, the terrain transforms into a wonderland of colors and textures. The cold air and softer light of winter enhance the natural beauty of the region, making it a magical time to forage in the wild, and not just because of Christmas!

The temperatures rarely dip below freezing in the deserts, but the plateaus, canyons, and mountains often experience heavy snowfall. This is a time when most plants lie dormant, but there are still a few good hidden gems you can forage for.

## The Terrain

In the winter season, the terrain undergoes a massive transformation. The region's vast deserts become more temperate, with cooler days and chilly nights. The usually scorching sun is softer, casting long shadows over the harsh terrain. The occasional winter rains can bring a subtle green flush to the arid ground, with wildflowers beginning to bloom in delicate colors.

The scene is even more transformative in the high plateaus and canyons. The Colorado Plateau is particularly striking in winter. The red rock formations and mesas are dusted with snow, creating a delightful contrast between the warm earth tones and the bright white snow. The Grand Canyon offers a breathtaking sight with its snow-capped rims and deep, multicolored rock layers.

The mountainous regions are blanketed in snow. Pine, spruce, and fir trees dominate the terrain, their branches heavy with white, creating a classic winter scene. However, the snow rarely reaches the base of the mountains, so the weather below is usually as mild as the deserts.

Rivers continue to flow, their banks framed by icy edges and snow-covered vegetation. The bare branches of deciduous trees stand in stark contrast to the evergreen shrubs, adding a touch of green to the predominantly white and brown environment.

## Availability of Plants

While the lush abundance of spring and fall might be absent, certain resilient and hardy plants continue to thrive in the moderate cold of winter in the Southwest. In the desert regions, you can find prickly pear cactus with its pads still available. However, it's the cholla cacti you need to look out for. Their flower buds grow in cold climates, which are highly nutritious. Creosote bush leaves, known for their medicinal properties, remain evergreen and can be foraged throughout the year.

Certain hardy plants, like wild onions and garlic, can be found near rivers and streams, providing flavorful additions to winter meals. Juniper berries ripen during this time, providing a flavorful addition to wild game dishes and herbal teas. Although the main harvest season is in the fall, some pinyon pine nuts can still be found lingering in the cones in the mountains. Oak trees also might still have some acorns available.

Back in the day, watercress (a type of flowering cabbage plant) was only found in Europe and Asia. These days, you can locate it near the flowing waters of rivers and streams in the Southwest. Essentially, if you know what to look for – and where – you can collect several bagfuls of edibles even in the dormant winter season. The key is to focus on hardy plants that withstand the colder temperatures and continue to provide edible parts throughout the season.

## Quick Tips and Precautions

- Although many parts of the Southwest don't experience snowfall throughout the winter, the climate is chilly, with temperatures often hovering around 30 degrees. Wear winter gear and clothing while heading out, including long-sleeved shirts, full pants, and gloves to protect against thorny plants.

- Avoid scaling mountain peaks for possible foraging opportunities to prevent hypothermia from seeping in. Travel to the plateaus and canyons instead if you are looking for an adventure and a cool view while foraging. Make sure you have enough layers to protect against the cold.

- If you are headed to the arid lands, equip yourself for the occasional rainfall. Carry a rain jacket or an umbrella, and stay near an elevated area in case of flash floods.

# Chapter 4: Wild Edible Plants of the Southwest

For centuries, early settlers relied on wild edible plants and herbs for food and medicine. Curious minds fascinated with the different benefits of wild plants made these discoveries possible. They took a leap of faith, recorded their observations, and passed on the knowledge to future generations.

There are plenty of edibles in the Southwest. [16]

In this chapter, you'll learn how to recognize wild edibles found in the Southwest, the best times and places to harvest them, and how to prepare them safely for consumption.

You'll get detailed descriptions to help you identify each plant and information on its traditional and modern uses. If you already enjoy foraging, these exciting and nutritious plants can be added to your foraging list.

# Edible Cacti in the Southwest

Before you read these plant profiles, remember that many desert plants, including most cacti, are slow-growing plants: a single cactus may take years or decades to reach maturity, and even longer to produce viable offspring. Individual cacti, populations, and whole plant communities are much slower to "bounce back" from disturbance, compared with forest or grassland plants. Many species of cactus across the Southwest have been seriously endangered by habitat destruction and overexploitation by humans – don't be part of the problem! When foraging cacti, take only the minimum you need, avoid damaging plants if possible, and if harvesting fruits or seeds, leave enough for wildlife and the persistence of the species.

### Prickly Pear Cactus (*Opuntia* spp.)

Prickly pears (*Opuntia* spp.) are among the most instantly recognizable cacti, with flat, paddle-shaped pads (*nopales*) and red or purple fruits (*tuna*), both edible and nutritious. Numerous species have been used as food for centuries by indigenous peoples across the continent, and remain essential ingredients in tradtional Mexican cuisine.

The desert prickly pear cactus (*Opuntia phaeacantha*), one of the most common species of prickly pear in the Southwest. [17]

### Identification

Prickly pears are best identified by their flat green stems or "paddles", which are armed with both large spines and smaller bristles called **glochids**. The large flowers are generally yellow, orange, or pink; the fruits, called *tuna* in Spanish, are green initially, ripening to a deep red or purple. The fruits have no spines but are armed with glochids, which must be sliced or scorched off before using the fruit.

### Uses

The paddles (*nopales* or *nopalitos*), once cleaned of spines, can be sliced into strips and eaten raw in salads or cooked and added to tacos, eggs, soups, or served alone as a side. The fruits can be eaten raw or made into preserves, syrup, and even a traditional wine known as *colonche*.

Be cautious when harvesting and always wear gloves when handling *nopales* or *tuna*, as the glochids can cause severe irritation and are difficult to remove.

### Barrel Cactus (*Ferocactus* spp.)

As the common name suggests, barrel cacti are stout and cylindrical in shape, similar to a barrel.

The barrel cactus. [18]

### Identification

Barrel cacti are squat and barrel-shaped, with prominent curved spines arranged in bundles along vertical ridges on the main stem. Bright yellow or red flowers appear from the top of the plant in late spring or early fall, depending on the species and habitat.

## Uses

The ripe fruits have a sweet, tangy flavor and can be eaten raw or cooked. Raw fruits should be consumed in moderation, as they contain oxalic acid that can interfere with calcium absorption, and in large quantities can cause kidney stones in some people. The seeds are about the size of poppy seeds and can be used similarly; they are also high in protein and can be used like amaranth or quinoa.

Some species of barrel cactus are rare or endangered in the wild due to overexploitation, especially by the nursery trade, so harvest sustainably: a good rule of thumb is one tenth of the fruits/seeds from a single plant or population.

## Cholla Cactus (*Cylindropuntia* spp.)

Cholla is related to prickly pear, but instead of flat paddles it has segmented, cylindrical joints.

The buckhorn cholla (*Cylindropuntia acanthocarpa*), a common species throughout most of the region. [19]

## Identification

Cholla often assumes a bushy or shrub-like form, with branching cylindrical stems with numerous spines. The flowers can be yellow, orange, or green.

## Uses

Cholla buds should be harvested before opening and either used immediately or dried for future use. The buds can be eaten raw, pickled, boiled or roasted and are delicious added to soups, stews and salads, or enjoyed alone. The stems can be cooked like prickly pear *nopales*, after the spines have been removed.

Cholla spines have rearward-facing barbs that make them painful and difficult to remove, so always use tongs or gloves (or both) when harvesting or handling, and ensure all spines are removed before use. Harvest the buds in early spring, or the stems throughout the spring and summer.

## Saguaro Cactus (*Carnegiea gigantea*)

The iconic saguaro cactus can reach up to 40 feet in height and live for centuries. Like many other cacti in the Southwest, it produces edible fruits, which require special equipment to harvest, especially on larger specimens.

The iconic saguaro cactus (Carnegiea gigantea). [20]

## Identification

The saguaro cactus is so distinctive and iconic in appearance as to be practically unmistakable: tall and columnar, older specimens often have classic upward-curving "arms", though younger individuals may lack these. Its white flowers bloom from the very top of the plant in late spring to early summer. The fruits, which emerge in June, look somewhat like prickly pears and turn deep purple when ripe.

## Uses

The ripe fruits can be eaten fresh, dried, or in syrup and preserves; the seeds can be dried, lightly roasted, and ground into a kind of flour that can be added to wheat flour in breads or made into a porridge similar to cream of wheat.

Use a long pole to knock down the ripe fruits; if possible, bring a friend to catch them so they don't burst when they hit the ground! The fruits ripen in early summer, but take care not to over-harvest: less than one percent of saguaro seedlings survive to maturity, so leave plenty for the next generation.

### Fishhook Cactus (*Mammillaria* and *Cochemiea* spp.)

These small, globular cacti, sometimes called "pincushion cacti", are named for their recurved, fishhook-like spines. Their flowers bloom in circular "haloes" near the top of the plants.

The fishhook cactus. [21]

### Identification

These small cacti are densely covered in spines that are usually hooked at the tip; the spines are borne in clusters of 5 or more at the tips of nipple-like *tubercules* along the main stem. The flowers are usually pink or red, and form a ring near (but not at) the top of the stem.

### Uses

The small, red fruits have a tangy flavor sometimes compared to strawberries, and can be eaten fresh or made into preserves, but they rarely appear in large quantities.

Handle with care to avoid the spines, and harvest only a few fruits from each plant you find. The fruits ripen in late summer.

### Organ Pipe Cactus (*Stenocereus thurberi*)

Found in the Sonoran Desert, the organ pipe cactus forms numerous cylindrical, unbranched stems from a central trunk, sometimes reaching 15-20 feet or more in height.

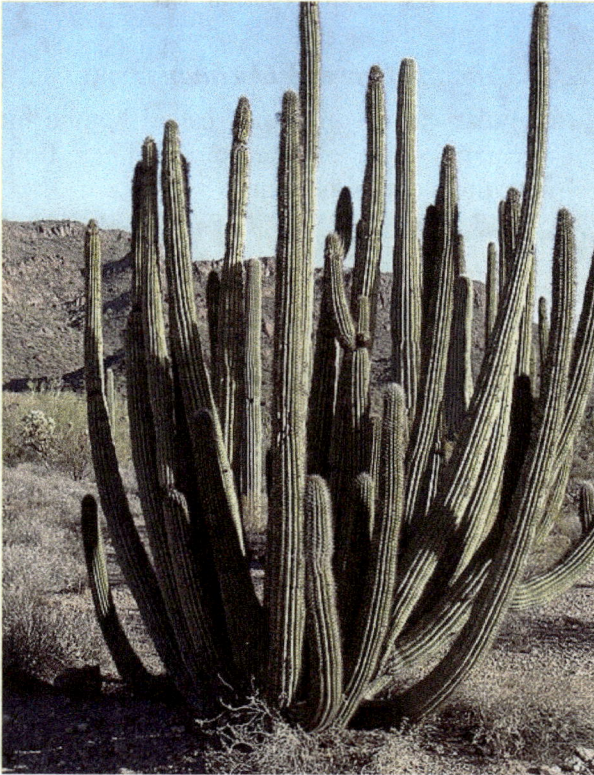

The organ pipe cactus (*Stenocereus thurberi*). [23]

### Identification

The tall, columnar stems rise from a single base. During its blooming period, it produces white flowers that open at night. The fruits are about the size of golf balls, covered in spines, and red or orange when ripe.

### Uses

The fruits can be dried, eaten fresh, or used in different deserts.

Similar to saguaro, you may need a pole or other implement to harvest organ pipe cactus fruits. Fruits ripen in late summer and should be handled with care (or better yet, tongs) as they are well-armed with spines.

# Edible Greens and Shoots in the Southwest

## Goosefoot (*Chenopodium* spp.)

Goosefoots (*Chenopodium* spp.) are closely related to quinoa (*C. quinoa*), as well as amaranth (*Amaranthus* spp.) and spinach (*Spinacia oleracea*). Though commonly considered weeds, both the greens and seeds of goosefoot are nutritional highly nutritious, and have been used as food by indigenous peoples and Europeans for centuries.

Lamb's quarters [38]

### Identification

Goosefoots are annuals, emerging in late spring. Most have diamond or lance-shaped leaves similar in shape to a goose's or duck's foot; the leaves are gray-green and often appear to have a dusty or floury coating (actually hair-like glands on the leaves), especially on new growth. Clusters of inconspicuous flowers with the same powdery texture emerge at the tips of the stems in mid-summer, followed by equally inconspicuous "fruits" – really just a seed with a paper-thin husk – in late summer or early fall.

### Uses

The greens can be eaten raw in salads, cooked like spinach, or added to soups and stews. The seeds must be husked and winnowed to remove the bitter coating, but once processed can be used just like quinoa, or popped and eaten like (minuscule) popcorn.

### Harvesting Tip

Harvest leaves in the spring and early summer; the uppermost or youngest leaves have the best flavor and texture, while older leaves become tough and stringy. The seeds can be harvested in the fall, after the plants have died, but must be processed (see above) before use.

### Purslane (*Portulaca oleracea*)

All parts of this succulent annual are edible: the leaves and stems have a mildly tangy flavor and are packed with omega-3 fatty acids and antioxidants.

Purslane (*Portulaca oleracea*). [*]

### Identification

The leaves are small and elliptical, generally widest closer to the tip; they are succulent, with a spongy texture and shiny, slightly leathery appearance. Like the leaves, the stems are thick and succulent, generally reddish in color and creeping or trailing; the flowers are small, yellow, and five-petaled, blooming throughout mid- to late summer.

## Uses

The leaves and stems can be eaten raw in salads, sautéed like spinach, or added to soups and stews; the mucilage in the leaves has a thickening effect somewhat like okra.

### Harvesting Tip

Purslane can be harvested throughout its growing season (early summer to fall), but only harvest from robust and healthy plants – avoid plants with shriveled leaves or stems, as these are signs of senescent (withering) or stressed plants, which are less palatable.

### Miner's Lettuce (*Claytonia perfoliata*)

Named for its use by California Gold Rush miners, Miner's lettuce is a healthy green that thrives in cool, moist conditions.

Miner's lettuce (*Claytonia perfoliate*). [25]

## Identification

Miner's lettuce is an annual, growing to about one foot in height and easily identified by its round upper leaves, which completely surround the stems. The lower leaves are long, narrow, and spatula-shaped, similar in appearance to baby lettuce (but smaller and more elongated). The five-petaled white flowers emerge in clusters above the leaves, blooming from January to July, depending on the location.

## Uses

Miner's lettuce has a mild, slightly sweet flavor that is excellent raw in salads or on sandwiches. Leaves and stems can be lightly sautéed with salt and pepper as a potherb, or added to soups and stews just before serving.

## Harvesting Tip

Harvest leaves and stems very early in spring before the plants flower, as young leaves have the best flavor.

## Wild Amaranth (*Amaranthus* spp.)

Amaranths and pigweeds are hardy plants in the same family as goosefoot and spinach. Amaranth was a nutritionally and culturally significant crop for indigenous peoples in the Southwest and Mexico, and its leaves and seeds are still staples in cultures across the world.

Palmer's amaranth (*Amaranthus palmeri*), one of the most abundant native wild amaranths in the Southwest. [26]

## Identification

Amaranths are mostly fast-growing summer annuals, emerging in late spring and living for only a few months. Most species can be easily identified by their relatively large size (3-5 feet tall) and pyramidal or "Christmas tree" shape. Their stems are fibrous, ribbed, and often reddish in color; the leaves are elliptical or lance-shaped, with long petioles – also often red-tinged – and tapering tips, frequently acquiring a slightly fuzzy texture as they age. The flowers are wind-pollinated and inconspicuous individually, but borne in distinctive crowded spikes at the tips of the stems. The fruits look much like the flowers to the untrained eye, and contain small black seeds somewhat like quinoa.

## Uses

Young leaves can be eaten fresh, but all species contain high levels of oxalic acid and should be eaten in moderation. New leaves and shoots can be cooked and used much like spinach in soups, omelettes, or as a side. Seeds can be used in granola or muesli, cooked like quinoa, or popped in a dry skillet and mixed with honey or syrup to make the traditional Mexican candy *alegria*.

## Harvesting Tip

Harvest young leaves and shoots (while still soft and flexible) in early summer, seeds in early fall when the plants die and dry out. Seeds must be hulled and winnowed thoroughly before use, as the husks contain bitter saponins.

## Nettles (*Urtica dioica*)

Stinging nettles may not strike most readers as "good eating", and it's true that all parts of the plant are covered in potentially painful stinging hairs. However, these hairs are easily removed by cooking or soaking, and once "disarmed" the greens are nutritious and delicious, with a fresh taste somewhat like spinach.

## Identification

Nettles are tall, slender perennials, with unbranched stems that can easily reach 4-5 feet high. The leaves are heart-shaped or teardrop-shaped, dark green, and sharply serrated; both leaves and stems are covered with tiny stinging hairs. The flowers are very small

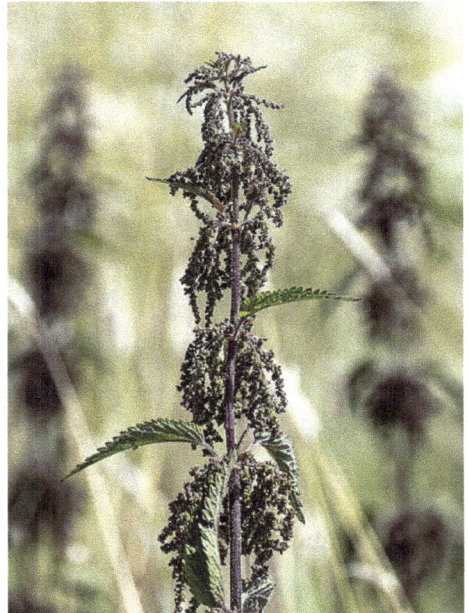

Stinging nettle (*Urtica dioica*).[17]

and white, borne in whorled clusters from the upper leaf axils (where the leaf attaches to the stem).

### Uses

Nettles must be cooked or soaked in cold water overnight to neutralize the formic acid responsible for their "sting". Once processed, they can be used in soups, stews, or eaten alone. They are particularly good with pasta, and can be added to pesto for a unique flavor.

### Harvesting Tip

Always wear thick gloves when harvesting to avoid stings. Harvest the youngest, highest leaves in early spring, before the plants get more than about waist high; older leaves are stringy and unpalatable.

### Dandelion (*Taraxacum officinale*)

Among the most common and widespread plants on Earth, dandelions are practically unmistakable, with bright yellow flowers that give way to fluffy, diaphanous seed heads.

Dandelion. [28]

### Identification

Dandelion leaves are lance-shaped and deeply lobed with large, backward-facing teeth; they radiate directly from the roots in a circular pattern called a **basal rosette**. The long taproots allow the plant to survive droughts and poor growing conditions, ensuring their bright yellow flowers return year after year.

### Uses

The leaves can be eaten raw in salads (in moderation, as they can be quite bitter depending on the plant) or used as a potherb like kale and collard greens. The flowers can be added to salads for a pop of color, or used to make wine, jelly, or syrup. The roots can be roasted, ground, and steeped for a chicory-like coffee substitute.

### Harvesting Tip

Harvest leaves in early spring before plants flower. Flowers should be harvested when fully open, and roots should be harvested in the fall. Avoid harvesting from agricultural fields, golf courses, and other areas where chemical pesticides may be used, as these can migrate into the plants.

### Woodsorrel (*Oxalis* spp.)

Woodsorrel is easily identified by its shamrock-like leaves, and its tart, lemony flavor is a perfect addition to spring salads.

Wood sorrel. [29]

### Identification

Woodsorrel has compound leaves with three heart-shaped leaflets and very long petioles; the flowers are small, five-petaled, and usually yellow or white – though one common species, violet woodsorrel (*O. violacea*), has pink or magenta flowers.

## Uses

The leaves and flowers can be added raw to salads or used as garnish; they are rich in oxalic acid (named for the genus) that lends a tangy flavor to dishes.

## Harvesting Tip

Various species of woodsorrel can be found throughout the Southwest, generally in grasslands or woodlands; leaves and flowers can be harvested whenever they are available, but should be eaten in moderation due to their oxalic acid content.

## Chickweed (*Stellaria media*)

This tender, mild-flavored green grows in cool, moist conditions.

Chickweed. [50]

## Identification

Chickweed leaves are small, oval, and paired along the stem, which has a line of fine hairs. The flowers are tiny, white, and star-shaped.

## Uses

You can eat them raw in salads, on sandwiches, or as a garnish. They can also be cooked in soups or stews.

## Harvesting Tip

Harvest tender young shoots and leaves in early spring. For the best flavor, avoid plants that have started to flower.

## Mallow (Malva *neglecta*)

It's a common plant with edible leaves, stems, and seeds.

Mallow. [81]

### Identification

Mallow has rounded leaves with shallow lobes and a slightly crinkled texture. The stem is covered with small hairs, and it produces small white flowers. The fruits are round and divided into pie slice-like segments.

### Uses

Leaves and stems can be consumed raw or cooked. Likewise, the seeds can be eaten fresh or dried.

### Harvesting Tip

Harvest young leaves and stems in spring and summer. Collect seeds in late summer.

# Edible Flowers in the Southwest

## Desert Marigold (Baileya multiradiata)

This is a bright yellow flower commonly found in desert regions, known for its vibrant petals and drought resistance.

Desert marigold. [88]

## Identification

The flowers are bright yellow and daisy-like, with numerous petals. The leaves are silvery green with a wooly texture. Under feasible conditions, the plant can grow up to two feet tall.

## Uses

The petals can add color and a slightly bitter flavor to salads and desserts.

## Harvesting Tip

Harvest flowers in the early morning when they are fresh. Rinse gently before use.

### Prickly Pear Cactus Flowers (*Opuntia* spp.)

These are large, showy flowers that bloom on the pads of prickly pear cacti.

Prickly pear cactus flowers. [88]

## Identification

The flowers on the prickly pear cactus grow directly on the cactus pads and can be yellow, red, or purple in color.

## Uses

The petals can be used fresh in salads, as a garnish, or dried for tea.

## Harvesting Tip

Use gloves to avoid the spines. Harvest flowers in full bloom and rinse gently before consumption and storage.

## Yucca Flowers (*Yucca* spp.)

Yucca plants have long and narrow leaves, which are leathery and usually tipped with spines. Related to agaves, they have their showy flowers are borne in large clusters at the tops of long spikes that can reach 10 feet high.

Yucca flowers. [84]

### Identification

The flowers are large and bell-shaped, white or cream in color, and grow in large clusters, whereas the leaves are long, narrow, and flexible, usually with a single sharp spine at the tip.

### Uses

Flowers can be eaten raw in salads, cooked in soups, or fried. They have a mild, slightly sweet flavor.

Harvesting Tips: Harvest flowers in the early morning when they are fresh. Remove any tough parts before use.

### Saguaro Cactus Flowers (*Carnegiea gigantea*)

The large, white blooms of the state flower of Arizona are iconic in the Sonoran Desert.

Saguaro cactus flowers. [85]

## Identification

The flowers are large, white, funnel-shaped, and have numerous petals. They grow on the cactus's arms.

## Uses

The petals can be eaten fresh or dried for tea. The flowers are also used to make jams and syrups.

## Harvesting Tip

Use a long pole to access flowers on tall cacti. Harvest in the early morning or late afternoon.

# Wild Berries in the Southwest

**Desert Hackberry (*Celtis pallida*)**

Desert hackberry is a small to medium-sized tree that produces bright orange, edible berries.

Desert hackberry. [86]

## Identification

Desert hackberry rarely grows above 10 to 15 feet in height. The leaves are small and elliptical, with faintly toothed margins, and the stems are armed with spines. The berries are small and bright orange when ripe.

## Uses

The berries can be eaten fresh, dried, or used in jams and jellies.

## Harvesting Tip

Harvest the berries when they are fully ripe in late summer to early fall.

## Wolfberry (*Lycium* spp.)

Goji berries or wolfberries are small, red, and highly nutritious.

Wolfberry. [87]

### Identification

The shrub can grow to a height of six feet, with narrow leaves, and produces red and oval berries that look a little like small chile peppers (*Capsicum annuum*). Most species have thorny stems, so use caution when harvesting.

### Uses

The berries can be eaten fresh, dried, or used in teas and soups. They are sweet and slightly tart.

### Harvesting Tip

Harvest the berries in late summer to early fall when they are fully red and plump.

### Chokecherry (*Prunus virginiana*)

This is a small tree or large shrub closely related to peaches (*P. persica*) and cherries (*P. avium*). It blooms prolifically in spring, with showy white flowers that give way to clusters of dark red to black edible berries.

Chokecherry. [88]

### Identification

Growing up to a height of 20 feet, chokecherry has distinctive blossoms, which form long, lilac-like clusters. The fruits, dark red to black berries, ripen in late summer.

### Uses

These berries make great jams, jellies, syrups, and wines. Due to their strong tartness and bitterness, they are generally not eaten fresh.

### Harvesting Tip

Harvest in late summer when the berries are fully dark and juicy.

### Elderberry (*Sambucus* spp.)

This is a shrub producing clusters of small, dark purple to black berries.

Elderberry. [39]

### Identification

Besides seeing berries growing, the leaves on the shrub have five to nine leaflets each.

### Uses

Make syrups, wines, jellies, and medicinal tinctures. They must be cooked before consumption.

### Harvesting Tip

Harvest in late summer to early fall when the berries are fully ripe and dark.

## Sumac (*Rhus* spp.)

A shrub producing clusters of red berries known for their tart flavor.

Sumac berries. [40]

### Identification

The red berries have fine hairs and serrated leaves.

### Uses

It is mostly used to make a tart, lemony drink called sumac-ade, and as a spice in Middle Eastern cuisine.

### Harvesting Tip

Harvest in late summer when the berries are fully red and tart.

# Nuts and Seeds in the Southwest

## Mesquite Pods (*Prosopis* spp.)

Mesquites are thorny shrubs or small trees common throughout the arid regions of western North America. They produce long "beans" or seed pods packed with a sweet and nutritious pulp, with a flavor somewhat like its distant cousin, tamarind (*Tamarindus indica*).

### Identification

Mesquite trees have feathery, compound leaves like those of acacias (*Acacia* spp.) and mimosas (*Mimosa* spp.), each with a pair of stout spines at its base. Most species flower in spring or early summer, with white flowers borne in long, fragrant clusters. The fruits look a little like flattened green beans and ripen in late summer, turning from bright green to light brown and often streaked with red or purple.

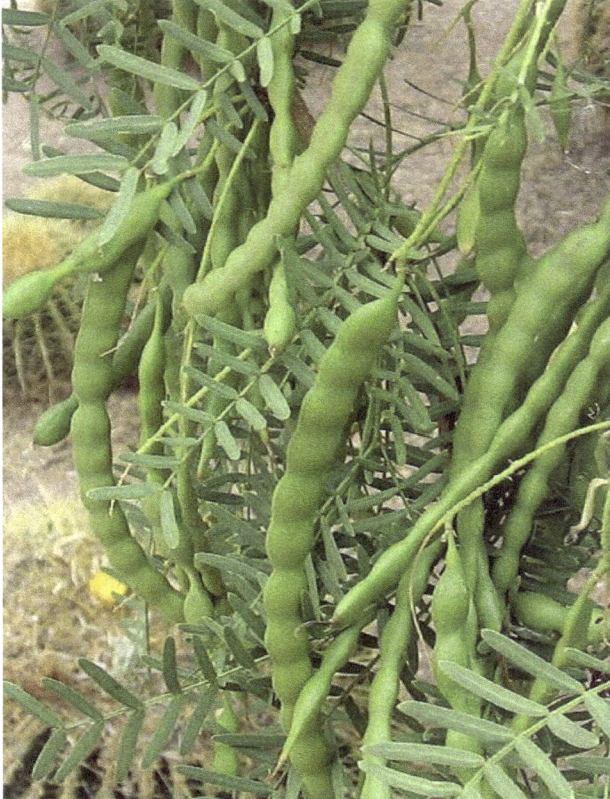

Pods and leaves of honey mesquite (*P. glandulosa*), common and widespread throughout the region. [41]

## Use

The whole pods can be dried, ground, and sifted to extract the sweet pulp, which can be used as a sweetener or a nutritious addition to baked goods by substituting for wheat flour in a 1:3 ratio.

### Harvesting Tip

Harvest pods when they are fully ripe and streaked with purple. If you're unsure what a ripe mesquite pod looks like, try a simple taste test: crack a pod open and taste the pulp: if it's sweet, it's ready to harvest!

### Pinyon Pine Nuts (*Pinus edulis*)

### Identification

Pinyons are some of the smallest and hardiest pines in North America, forming extensive open woodlands in the high, cool deserts of the Great Basin. The small, round cones of pinyons contain large edible seeds with a rich, buttery flavor similar to European pine nuts but sweeter.

Pinyon pine nut.[a]

## Uses

The nuts can be eaten raw or roasted, used whole or ground into meal and added to baked goods. They are rich in protein, healthy fats, and a number of micronutrients.

### Harvesting Tip

Harvest the nuts when they are fully mature, and fall easily from their cones. You may need to use a pole to reach cones on higher trees, and you'll likely be competing with birds, chipmunks, deer, and even bears – so make sure to leave plenty for your neighbors. The seeds have thin, hard shells that must be cracked and removed before consumption.

## Acorns (*Quercus* spp.)

### Identification

Acorns are the instantly recognizable fruits of oak trees (*Quercus*), which are among the most widespread trees on the continent. They're energy-rich, plentiful, and readily consumed by most animals – including humans! However, most acorns contain high concentrations of tannins, intensely bitter chemicals that must be leached before eating.

Gambel's oak (Quercus gambelii), one of the most widely harvested species in the Southwest. Note the rounded lobes on the leaves, characteristic of oaks with low-tannin acorns. [48]

### Uses

Once they have been processed, acorns can be boiled, roasted, or ground into flour, which adds a nutty flavor and nutritional punch to pancakes and baked goods.

### Harvesting Tip

Only harvest acorns from oaks with round-lobed leaves – the so-called "white oaks". The acorns of red oaks, which have bristle-tipped leaves, are much higher in tannins, and often unpalatably bitter even after extensive processing. Harvest the acorns as soon as possible after they begin fall from the trees, and inspect them carefully for holes or cracks – these likely indicate spoilage or insect infestation. To leach the tannins, simmer the acorns in an uncovered pot until the water starts to take on the color of tea, then dump and pour in fresh water; do this until the water stays clear.

# Jojoba Seeds (*Simmondsia chinensis*)

Jojoba nuts. "

## Identification

Jojoba is a large, leggy shrub with gray-green, leathery leaves arranged in opposite pairs on the stems. The flowers are yellow-green, small and relatively inconspicuous, blooming in late spring and ripening over the summer into pendulous fruits that look a little like uncured olives, each with a large dark-brown seed.

## Uses

The seeds are pressed to extract their oil, which is widely used in cosmetic and skin care products, and has been used medicinally by indigenous peoples throughout the region.

## Harvesting Tip

Harvest the seeds when they are fully ripe and the outer shell has begun to shrivel and wrinkle. Crack open the shells to extract the oily seeds inside.

# Golden Chia (*Salvia columbariae*)

Golden chia in bloom. "

## Identification

Golden chia is a hardy annual plant in the mint family, that produces tiny seeds that swell when soaked in liquid. Found throughout the Southwest, from Southern California to New Mexico, it's easily recognized by its deeply compound opposite leaves, square stems, and purple flowers, which form distinctive spherical clusters.

## Uses

The seeds can be eaten raw or ground into flour, which can be used in baked goods or added to smoothies. They are an excellent source of dietary fiber, as well as omega-3 fatty acids.

## Harvesting Tip

Harvest seeds when the flower clusters turn a golden-brown and begin to dry out in late summer. Clip the heads just below the lowest flowers, then toss the whole head into a paper bag, Allow these to dry for a few days, then shake thoroughly to separate the seeds from the flower heads. Store in a cool, dry place.

# Roots and Tubers in the Southwest

## Breadroot (*Pediomelum* spp.)

Indian potato. "

### Identification

Breadroot, sometimes called scurf pea, is a genus of plants in the same family (Fabaceae) as green beans (*Phaseolus* spp.) and garden lupines (*Lupinus* spp.), with a similar appearance to the latter; they are easily recognized by their palmately compound leaves and purple or lilac flowers. Many species produce edible tubers, which have been used both as food and medicine by many cultures throughout the continent.

### Uses

The roots are edible raw, boiled, or roasted like other root vegetables, or dried and ground into flour that can be added to wheat flour in baked goods. They have a pleasant, nutty flavor and are rich in protein and carbohydrates.

### Harvesting Tip

Harvest the roots in the fall just before the aboveground parts die back. Wash and peel before cooking.

# Wild Onion (*Allium* spp.)

Desert onion (A. macropetalum), one of the few species of wild onion that thrives in desert habitats. [47]

## Identification

Although wild onions (*Allium* spp.) are often associated with woodlands and stream banks, a number of species are common in the Southwes in a wide range of habitats, from riverbanks and montane forests to the deserts of southern Arizona and New Mexico. All have long, narrow leaves, similar to grass but with a slightly succulent texture. and have a pungent garlic or onion smell when crushed. Always check for this smell before harvesting, as it is a reliable way to distinguish edible species from toxic lookalikes like death camas (*Toxicoscordion*).

## Uses

Wild onion bulbs and bulblets taste a little like a cross between scallions and garlic, and can be substituted for either. The greens have a more delicate flavor and can be added to salads and dips or as a garnish like chives.

## Harvesting Tip

Harvest greens at any time; harvest bulbs after plants have fully bloomed or set seed. Some (but not all) species also produce pea-sized "bulblets" on their flowering stalks; these generally appear in spring or early summer, and have a similar flavor to the bulbs.

# Sunchoke (*Helianthus tuberosus*)

Sunchoke. [48]

## Identification

Sunchokes are members of the daisy family (Asteraceae), similar in appearance to the common annual sunflower (*H. annuus*). Unlike their cousins, sunchokes are perennial plants, storing energy in knobby, potato-like tubers. Sunchokes can be identified by their leaves – which are longer and narrower than common sunflower leaves – and by their flowers, which are a bit smaller than common sunflowers and have yellow rather than black centers.

## Uses

The tubers can be sliced and eaten raw or cooked like potatoes with a sweet and nutty flavor reminiscent of artichoke hearts.

## Harvesting Tip

Harvest the tubers any time outside of the growing season, from fall to early spring, as this is when they are sweetest and most tender. Wash and scrub thoroughly before use.

# Biscuitroot (*Lomatium* spp.)

Desert parsley. [49]

## Identification

Desert parsley, sometimes called biscuitroot, is a cousin of the carrot (*Daucus carota*) and the parsnip (*Pastinaca* spp.), and shares the feathery, highly compound foliage characteristic of its family (Apiaceae). True to its name, desert parsley thrives in arid and unforgiving climates, thanks to a long, deep – and edible – taproot. Most common species also have strongly scented leaves, which can be used just like a couple of other relatives, parsley (*Petroselinum crispum*) and cilantro (*Coriandrum sativum*).

## Uses

The roots can be eaten raw or cooked and have a peppery, parsley-like flavor. The plant's name derives from the traditional method of processing: roots were roasted or dried, then ground into a kind of "flour" that could be stored for long periods. The leaves can be used as a seasoning or garnish.

## Harvesting Tip

Harvest the roots in the fall or early spring before the plants break dormancy; once the growing season starts, the taproots gradually exhaust the stored sugars and starches, becoming tough and unpalatable.

## Desert Lily (*Hesperocallis undulata*)

Desert lily. [50]

### Identification

Desert lilies are quite striking in appearance, especially when in bloom: their large, luxuriant white blooms are an odd contrast to the baking heat and desolation of the hot deserts in which they thrive. Their leaves, long and narrow like other plants in their family (Liliaceae), have distinctive "ruffled" or "wavy" margins, which help identify the plant at any time of year. These plants survive their harsh environmental conditions with the help of belowground storage organs (bulbs) that are a great source of energy for people too. The bulbs are covered in a thin brown skin, but the flesh inside is as white as the flowers.

### Uses

The roots can be boiled, mashed, roasted, or baked, and have a slightly sweet flavor that is enhanced by roasting and baking, which caramelizes the sugars in the bulbs. This method was traditional among Indigenous peoples in what is now California and Arizona .

### Harvesting Tip

Harvest the roots in the fall and throughout the winter, after the plant has died back and before it breaks dormancy in spring. Wash and peel before cooking.

## Sego Lily Bulbs (*Calochortus nuttallii*)

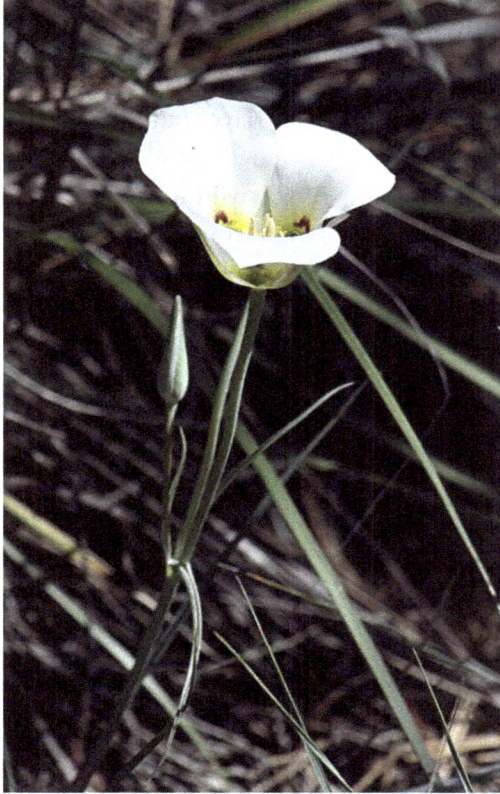

Sego lily. [51]

### Identification

The large, eye-catching blooms of sego lilies are distinctive and easy to recognize: three broad white petals alternate with narrower sepals, each with a purple streak at the base. (Some plants may have all pink or purple flowers.) The flowers may look delicate, but sego lilies are actually quite hardy, thriving in dry scrub and high desert thanks to its edible bulbs. The bulbs are white or yellowish and wrapped in a thin brown skin, and both the flowering stalk and the long, grass-like leaves emerge from the top.

### Uses

The bulbs have a slightly sweet flavor, particularly after roasting; they can also be boiled, fried, or mashed liked potatoes. Traditionally, they were harvested in large quantites and roasted in huge, charcoal-lined pits. The flowers and green seed pods are also edible, with a fresh "green" flavor sometimes compared to sweet peas.

## Harvesting Tip

Harvest the bulbs in the fall, just after the plants finish blooming but before the spent blooms fall from the plants; this well help distinguish them from lookalikes. If necessary, mark plants in advance so you can find them again after the flowers have faded. Wash and peel before cooking.

This was a general overview of the wild edibles found in the Southwest. To achieve the best foraging experience, spend time learning more about each species, remember the distinct features that make it easier to identify these plants, and always use safe foraging and consumption practices.

# Chapter 5: Mushrooms of the Southwest

The fascinating world of mushrooms of the Southwest checks all the boxes for any forager. This chapter will introduce you to the remarkable diversity and ecological significance of these often-overlooked organisms. Fungi are critical in forest ecosystems, assisting in nutrient cycling, soil formation, and symbiotic relationships with plants. Keep reading to know the complex and intriguing world of fungi and appreciate their beauty, diversity, and role in maintaining the ecosystem.

Fungi are critical in forest ecosystems. Mushroom. [53]

# The Ecological Importance of Fungi

## Decomposers

Fungi are vital decomposers in forest ecosystems. They break down dead organic matter, recycling nutrients back into the soil. This decomposition process maintains soil fertility and structure, releasing nutrients that plants need to grow. Without fungi, dead plant and animal matter would accumulate, and the nutrients within them would remain locked away, unavailable to other organisms.

### Symbiotic Relationships

Many fungi form mutualistic relationships with plants, particularly through structures known as mycorrhizae. Mycorrhizal fungi colonize plant roots and help the plant's ability to absorb water and nutrients, especially phosphorus. In return, the plants provide the fungi with carbohydrates produced through photosynthesis. This symbiosis is vital for the health and growth of many plant species, and it plays a significant role in forest health and productivity.

### Disease Control

While some fungi are pathogens that cause diseases in plants and animals, they also contribute to ecological balance by controlling populations. Pathogenic fungi can regulate the populations of certain species, preventing any one species from dominating the ecosystem. This helps maintain biodiversity and promotes a healthy, balanced ecosystem.

The next section of this chapter introduces specific fungi and mushrooms that thrive in the Southwest, each with unique characteristics and environmental contributions.

# Basic Mushroom Terminology

Understanding the anatomy and terminology of mushrooms is key to accurate identification and safe foraging. Mushrooms, the fruiting bodies of fungi, exhibit various shapes, sizes, and colors, making identification both fascinating and challenging. Here, you'll read the detailed anatomy of mushrooms and essential terms used in mushroom identification.

### Cap (Pileus)

The cap, or pileus, is the top part of the mushroom and is umbrella-shaped, although it can take many forms, like convex, flat, or bell-shaped. The surface of the cap can be smooth, scaly, sticky, or dry. Its color and texture are often crucial identification features.

## Key Terms

**Convex:** Rounded cap, like a dome.

**Flat:** A cap that is level on top.

**Umbonate:** Having a raised, knob-like center.

**Depressed:** Cap with a sunken center.

## Gills (Lamellae)

Located on the underside of the cap, gills are thin, blade-like structures that radiate outward from the stem. They produce and release spores, which are crucial for the fungus's reproduction. Gills can be free (not attached to the stem), adnexed (narrowly attached), adnate (broadly attached), or decurrent (running down the stem).

## Key Terms

**Free:** Gills not attached to the stem.

**Adnate:** Gills broadly attached to the stem.

**Decurrent:** Gills running down the length of the stem.

## Stem (Stipe)

The stem, or stipe, supports the cap and elevates it above the ground. Stems can vary greatly in length, thickness, and texture. Some mushrooms, like certain polypores, lack a stem altogether.

## Key Terms

**Equal:** Stem is the same width throughout.

**Tapered:** Stem narrows toward the base or cap.

**Bulbous:** Stem has a swollen base.

## Ring (Annulus)

The ring, or annulus, is a remnant of the partial veil that initially covered the gills or pores. Not all mushrooms have a ring, but their presence and characteristics (location and size) are important for identification.

## Key Terms

**Persistent:** The ring remains intact as the mushroom matures.

**Evanescent:** The ring disappears as the mushroom ages.

### Volva

The volva is a cup-like structure at the base of the stem – a remnant of the universal veil that enclosed the entire mushroom when it was young. It's particularly prominent in species like Amanita. The presence, shape, and size of the volva are critical for identification.

### Key Terms

**Saccate:** Sack-like volva.

**Lobed:** Volva with distinct lobes or segments.

# Importance of Accurate Identification and Caution in Foraging

Accurate mushroom identification is necessary to avoid consuming toxic species. Many edible mushrooms have toxic look-alikes that can cause serious illness or death. Proper identification involves examining multiple features, including cap shape, gill attachment, stem characteristics, and spore print color. Using a reliable field guide and cross-referencing with multiple sources is recommended.

### Potential Risks of Foraging

Foraging for wild mushrooms carries significant risks due to toxic species. Some common dangers include:

- Species like the Amanita phalloides (Death Cap) contain potent toxins that can cause severe poisoning and even death.

- Some people may have allergic reactions to certain mushrooms, even if they are generally considered safe to eat.

- Novice foragers may mistake toxic mushrooms for edible ones due to similarities in appearance.

### Safe Foraging Practices

- Learn from experienced foragers and take courses on mushroom identification.

- Always carry a reliable field guide specific to your region.

- Perform spore print tests to help with identification.

- Never assume a mushroom is edible based on appearance alone.

By understanding the anatomy and terminology of mushrooms and emphasizing accurate identification, you can safely enjoy the rewarding experience of mushroom foraging. Always approach foraging with caution and respect for the natural world.

# Tips for Mushroom Identification

Mushroom identification is a skill that requires careful observation, practice, and the use of multiple resources. Accurate identification is critical for safe foraging, as many mushrooms have toxic look-alikes. Below are detailed tips and techniques for distinguishing between edible, inedible, and poisonous species.

### Observe the Mushroom's Habitat

The habitat where a mushroom is found can provide important clues for identification. Different species prefer different environments:

**Forests:** Many mushrooms grow in wooded areas, often associated with specific tree species.

**Grasslands:** Some mushrooms, like puffballs, prefer open fields and meadows.

**Decaying Wood:** Many fungi decompose dead wood and can be found on fallen logs or stumps.

Knowing the preferred habitat of specific mushrooms can narrow down the possibilities.

### Examine the Cap (Pileus)

The cap is one of the most distinctive features of a mushroom:

**Shape:** Identify whether the cap is convex, flat, bell-shaped, or umbonate.

**Surface:** Note if the cap is smooth, scaly, sticky, or dry.

**Color:** Record the cap color, noting any color changes that occur as the mushroom ages.

**Margin:** Look at the edge of the cap to see if it is smooth, wavy, or has remnants of a veil.

### Inspect the Gills (Lamellae)

Gills are crucial for identifying many mushrooms:

**Attachment:** Check if the gills are free, adnexed, adnate, or decurrent.

**Color:** Note the color of the gills, which can change as the mushroom matures.

**Spacing:** Observe whether the gills are crowded, spaced, or forked.

### Study the Stem (Stipe)

The stem provides additional identification features.

**Length and Thickness:** Measure the length and thickness of the stem.

**Texture:** Note if the stem is smooth, fibrous, or scaly.

**Color:** Record the color and any color changes, including bruising.

**Presence of Ring:** Look for a ring (annulus) around the stem and describe its characteristics.

**Base:** Check for a bulbous base or volva, which is crucial for identifying certain toxic species.

### Take a Spore Print

A spore print is a key identification tool.

**Cap Placement:** Place the mushroom cap (gills down) on a piece of white and black paper or foil.

**Cover:** Cover the cap with a bowl or cup to prevent airflow.

**Wait:** Leave it for several hours or overnight.

**Examine:** Check the color of the spores that have fallen. Common spore print colors include white, brown, black, and pink.

### Smell and Taste (With Caution)

The smell and taste can provide additional clues, but tasting should only be done by experienced foragers and never with unknown species.

**Smell:** Some mushrooms have distinctive odors, like the anise scent of the anise mushroom (Clitocybe odora).

**Taste:** If tasting, chew a small piece and then spit it out. Do not swallow. This technique should be used with extreme caution and knowledge.

# Techniques for Distinguishing Edible, Inedible, and Poisonous Species

### Edible Species

Start by learning a few well-known, easily recognizable edible mushrooms, like chanterelles (Cantharellus spp.), morels (Morchella spp.), and puffballs (Lycoperdon spp.). Focus on distinctive features, like the false gills of chanterelles or the honeycomb caps of morels.

### Inedible Species

Some mushrooms, like certain polypores, are not toxic but inedible due to their tough texture or unpleasant taste. Learn to recognize these by their common names and distinguishing features to avoid confusing them with edibles.

### Poisonous Species

Many poisonous mushrooms closely resemble edible ones. For example, the Death Cap (Amanita phalloides) resembles some edible Amanita species. Pay close attention to key features like the volva at the base of Amanita species or the color changes in the gills of poisonous Cortinarius species. Never consume a mushroom unless you are 100% certain of its identity.

# Importance of Using Multiple Sources for Verification

Use field guides tailored to your geographical area, as mushroom species can vary by region. Good field guides include detailed illustrations and photographs to help with identification. Look for guides that comprehensively describe habitat, appearance, and key distinguishing features.

Here are some field guides that you can use:

- Southwest Foraging: 117 Wild and Flavorful Edibles from Barrel Cactus to Wild Oregano
- Wild Edible Plants of the Southwest: Locate, Identify, Store, and Prepare Your Foraged Finds
- Texas Edible Wild Plant Foraging: Beginner Foraging Field Guide for Finding, Identifying, Harvesting, and Preparing Edible Wild Food

### Local Mycological Societies

Join local mycological societies where you can learn from experienced foragers and mycologists. Participate in group forays to learn hands-on identification techniques. Attend workshops and lectures to deepen your knowledge and stay updated on new findings.

Mushroom identification is a rewarding but complex skill that requires careful observation, practice, and the use of multiple resources. Always approach foraging with caution and respect, ensuring you positively identify each mushroom before considering consumption.

### Safety Considerations in Mushroom Foraging

Wild mushrooms can be enjoyable and rewarding, but they also come with significant safety considerations. Proper identification is crucial, as many mushrooms have toxic look-alikes that can cause serious illness or death. Additionally, responsible foraging practices are vital for minimizing environmental impact and ensuring the sustainability of mushroom populations. Here's a detailed guide to safety and responsibility in mushroom foraging.

### Importance of Proper Identification

Accurate identification of mushrooms is the most critical aspect of safe foraging. Misidentification can lead to consuming toxic species with potentially fatal consequences. Here are key points to consider:

### Learning from Experts

Start by foraging with experienced mushroom hunters or mycologists. Learning from experts can help you understand the subtle differences between species. Enroll in local courses or workshops on mushroom identification. Many mycological societies offer these educational opportunities.

### Using Reliable Resources

Use high-quality field guides specific to your region. These guides provide detailed descriptions and illustrations to help with identification. Always cross-reference information from several sources, including field guides, online databases, and mycological societies.

### Detailed Observation

Note the environment where the mushroom is growing. Different species have specific habitat preferences, like forests, grasslands, or decaying wood. Carefully observe the cap, gills, stem, and other features. Pay attention to color, shape, size, texture, and any distinctive markings. Perform a spore print test to determine the spore color, which is an important identification characteristic. Only experienced foragers should use taste for identification and never swallow any part of an unknown mushroom. Some mushrooms have distinctive odors that can aid identification.

### Avoiding Toxic Look-Alikes

Many Amanita mushrooms are highly toxic. Key features include a volva at the base, white gills, and a ring on the stem. Learn to recognize these features. These genera contain deadly species. Be cautious with small brown mushrooms and those with rusty-colored spores. These mushrooms resemble true morels but are toxic. They have irregular, brain-like caps compared to the honeycomb pattern of true morels.

# Responsible Foraging Practices

To forage responsibly and sustainably, consider the following guidelines:

### Environmental Impact

Harvest mushrooms carefully to minimize damage to the surrounding ecosystem. Avoid trampling vegetation and disturbing the soil. Never harvest all the mushrooms in a given area. Leaving some behind ensures the species can continue to reproduce and thrive. Take only what you need. Overharvesting can deplete local mushroom populations and harm the ecosystem.

### Legal Considerations

Check local regulations regarding mushroom foraging. Some areas require permits or have restrictions on the amount you can collect. Always obtain permission before foraging on private property.

### Safety Precautions

Inform someone of your foraging plans, including your location and expected return time. Carry a map, compass, or GPS device. Wear appropriate clothing, including long sleeves and pants, to protect against insect bites and thorny plants. Use gloves when handling unknown mushrooms. Do not forage in areas that may be contaminated with pesticides, heavy metals, or other pollutants, like near roadsides or industrial sites.

### Ethical Considerations

Be mindful of the local wildlife. Avoid disrupting habitats and nesting sites. Share knowledge about sustainable foraging practices with others. Encourage respect for nature and responsible harvesting.

### Handling and Consumption

Store foraged mushrooms in a breathable container like a basket or paper bag. Avoid using plastic bags, as they can cause mushrooms to spoil. Clean mushrooms thoroughly to remove dirt and insects. Some mushrooms require specific preparation methods to be safe for consumption. When trying a new mushroom, eat a small amount first and wait 24 hours to check for any adverse reactions. This precaution helps identify any potential allergies or sensitivities.

# Profiles of Common Edible Mushrooms Found in the Southwest

Foraging for wild mushrooms in the Southwest can be a delightful experience, given the region's diverse array of edible fungi. However, it is crucial to exercise caution and proper identification skills, particularly with species that have toxic look-alikes. Below are detailed profiles of common edible mushrooms found in the Southwest, including essential identification features and cautionary notes.

### Desert Shaggy Mane (*Coprinus comatus*)

The desert shaggy mane, also known as the lawyer's wig or saggy ink cap, is a distinctive and easily recognizable mushroom.

Desert Shaggy Mane. [58]

### Identification

**Cap:** Cylindrical when young, expanding to bell-shaped. The cap is covered with white, shaggy scales.

**Gills:** White at first, turning black and liquifying as the mushroom matures (deliquescence).

**Stem:** Long, white, and hollow with a fibrous texture.

**Spore Print:** Black.

**Habitat:** Found in grasslands, open woods, and disturbed areas like roadsides and lawns, often appearing after rain.

**Edibility:** Best consumed when young, before the gills start to blacken. Cook promptly after harvesting as they do not store well.

**Caution:** Ensure proper identification, as some inedible species can look similar, especially when past their prime.

### Agaricus species

The Agaricus genus includes many edible species like the Meadow Mushroom (Agaricus campestris) and the Prince (Agaricus augustus).

Agaricus species. [54]

### Identification

**Cap:** White to brown, smooth or slightly scaly, usually convex to flat.

**Gills:** Pink when young, turning chocolate brown to black with age.

**Stem:** Sturdy with a ring (annulus) present. Some species have a bulbous base.

**Spore Print:** Chocolate brown.

**Habitat:** Found in grasslands, gardens, and woodlands, often in nutrient-rich soil.

**Edibility:** Many species are highly prized for their flavor, particularly when young and fresh.

**Caution:** Some Agaricus species, like Agaricus xanthodermus (Yellow Stainer), are toxic and can cause gastrointestinal upset. When bruised, they often have a chemical or phenol-like odor.

### Laccaria laccata

Commonly known as the Deceiver, Laccaria laccata is a small, edible mushroom.

Laccaria laccata. [55]

### Identification

**Cap:** Reddish-brown, smooth, and often hygrophanous (changing color as it loses moisture), ranging from convex to flat.

**Gills:** Thick, widely spaced, and the same color as the cap or paler.

**Stem:** Slender, tough, and fibrous, matching the cap color.

**Spore Print:** White to pale pink.

**Habitat:** Found in mixed woodlands, often forming mycorrhizal relationships with trees.

**Edibility:** Edible but not highly sought after due to its small size and relatively bland taste.

---

**Caution:** Ensure correct identification, as its variable appearance can make it confusing, especially for beginners.

### Puffballs (Various Genera)

Puffballs are a group of mushrooms that include genera like Lycoperdon and Calvatia.

Puffballs. [56]

### Identification

**Cap:** Round, without a distinct stem, and varies in size from small to large (e.g., Giant Puffball).

**Surface:** Smooth to spiky, turning from white to brown as they mature.

**Interior:** White and firm when young, turning yellowish and then brown as spores develop.

**Habitat:** Found in grasslands, forests, and disturbed areas, often appearing in fairy rings.

**Edibility:** Only edible when the interior is pure white and firm. Giant Puffballs (Calvatia gigantea) are particularly prized.

**Caution:** Avoid any puffballs with a mature brown or greenish interior, as they are inedible. Also, be cautious of immature Amanita mushrooms, which can resemble puffballs when young.

## Morchella species (Morels)

Morels are highly sought after for their distinctive appearance and exquisite flavor.

Morchella species. [57]

### Identification

**Cap:** Honeycomb or net-like pattern, with ridges and pits, ranging from light tan to dark brown.

**Stem:** Pale, hollow, and attached at the base of the cap.

**Spore Print:** Cream to light yellow.

**Habitat:** Found in forests, often near ash, elm, and apple trees, especially in disturbed soils and areas recently burned by wildfire.

**Edibility:** Highly prized for their nutty flavor and texture, excellent in a variety of dishes.

**Caution:** False morels (Gyromitra spp.) are toxic and can be mistaken for true morels. False morels often have a more irregular, lobed, or wrinkled cap and a chambered stem. True morels have a completely hollow stem.

## Chanterelles (Cantharellus cibarius and other species)

Chanterelles are prized for their fruity aroma and excellent culinary qualities.

Chanterelle. [58]

### Identification

**Cap:** Yellow to orange, funnel-shaped, with wavy edges.

**Gills:** False gills (ridges) that are forked and run down the stem.

**Stem:** Solid, matching the color of the cap.

**Spore Print:** Pale yellow to white.

**Habitat:** Found in mixed woodlands, often under oaks and conifers, during the monsoon season.

**Edibility:** Highly valued for their nutty flavor and firm texture, used in a variety of dishes.

**Caution:** Beware of toxic look-alikes like the Jack-o'-Lantern mushroom (Omphalotus olearius), which has true gills and a bioluminescent glow in the dark.

Beware of toxic look-alikes like this Jack-o'-Lantern mushroom. [59]

## Oyster Mushrooms (Pleurotus ostreatus and related species)

Oyster mushrooms are known for their delicate flavor and versatile use in cooking.

Oyster mushroom. [60]

### Identification

**Cap:** White to gray or brown, fan-shaped, and smooth.

**Gills:** White to cream, decurrent (running down the stem).

**Stem:** Often short or absent. If present, it is off-center.

**Spore Print:** White to lilac-gray.

**Habitat:** Found on dead or dying hardwood trees, often growing in clusters.

**Edibility:** Popular for their mild, anise-like flavor and tender texture.

**Caution:** Ensure identification as some similar-looking species can cause gastrointestinal upset.

### King Bolete (Boletus edulis)

Also known as Porcini, this mushroom is highly sought after for its robust flavor.

King bolete. [61]

### Identification

**Cap:** Brown, convex, with a smooth or slightly wrinkled surface.

**Pores:** White when young, turning yellow to olive with age.

**Stem:** Thick, club-shaped, often with a net-like pattern (reticulation).

**Spore Print:** Olive-brown.

**Habitat:** Found in mixed woodlands, particularly under pine, spruce, and oak trees.

**Edibility:** Renowned for its robust, earthy flavor, excellent in soups, stews, and pasta dishes.

**Caution:** Be cautious of toxic look-alikes like the Bitter Bolete (Tylopilus felleus), which has a very bitter taste.

Be cautious of toxic look-alikes like the Bitter Bolete.⁶²

## Chicken of the Woods (Laetiporus sulphureus and related species)

Known for its meaty texture and chicken-like taste.

Chicken of the woods. ⁶³

## Identification

**Cap:** Bright orange to yellow, shelf-like, with a smooth or slightly wrinkled surface.

**Pores:** Yellow, found on the underside of the cap.

**Stem:** Often absent, with the mushroom growing directly from wood.

**Spore Print:** White.

**Habitat:** Grows on dead or dying trees, particularly oak and other hardwoods.

**Edibility:** Popular as a chicken substitute in vegetarian dishes.

**Caution:** Some people may experience gastrointestinal upset with this mushroom. Ensure it is growing on hardwood, as those on conifers can cause adverse reactions.

### Black Trumpet (Craterellus cornucopioides)

Also known as the Horn of Plenty, these mushrooms are prized for their rich, smoky flavor.

Black trumpet. "

## Identification

**Cap:** Dark brown to black, funnel-shaped, with a wrinkled surface.

**Gills:** Lacks true gills but instead has a smooth or slightly wrinkled underside.

**Stem:** Often indistinguishable from the cap.

**Spore Print:** White.

**Habitat:** Found in deciduous woodlands, often under oak and beech trees, in moist, mossy areas.

**Edibility:** Highly valued for their deep, earthy flavor, excellent in sauces and soups.

**Caution:** Ensure proper identification, as their dark color can make them difficult to spot and easy to confuse with other fungi.

### Lion's Mane (Hericium erinaceus)

This unique mushroom is known for its shaggy appearance and seafood-like flavor.

Lion's mane. [65]

## Identification

**Cap:** White, consisting of long, spiny projections (teeth).

**Gills:** Absent, replaced by downward-growing spines.

**Stem:** Absent or rudimentary.

**Spore Print:** White.

**Habitat:** Found on hardwoods, particularly oak, beech, and maple.

**Edibility:** Prized for its delicate, lobster-like flavor and medicinal properties.

**Caution:** It is easy to identify due to its distinctive appearance, but ensure it is fresh and white, as older specimens can turn yellow and become inedible.

### Hedgehog Mushroom (Hydnum repandum)

Known for its tooth-like spines under the cap and excellent flavor.

Hedgehog mushroom. [66]

### Identification

**Cap:** Yellow to orange-brown, irregularly shaped, and slightly depressed in the center.

**Spines:** Tooth-like projections on the underside, white to yellow.

**Stem:** Short, stout, matching the cap color.

**Spore Print:** White.

**Habitat:** Found in mixed woodlands, often under conifers and hardwoods.

**Edibility:** Valued for its nutty, sweet flavor and firm texture.

**Caution:** It is easy to identify due to its spines, but it should not be confused with other toothed fungi.

# General Cautionary Notes

Foraging for wild mushrooms demands precise identification to avoid toxic species. Always cross-reference multiple sources and consider consulting with experienced foragers or mycologists. When in doubt, do not consume the mushroom.

### Responsible Foraging Practices

Pick mushrooms responsibly, leaving enough behind to ensure future growth and reproduction. Avoid disturbing habitats more than necessary, adhere to local regulations, and respect private property. Obtain necessary permits if required.

By following these guidelines and exercising caution, you can safely enjoy the diverse and delicious mushrooms that the Southwest has to offer.

# Chapter 6: Cooking Wild Edibles: 16 Delicious Recipes

Prepare tasty dishes using the mushrooms, roots, berries, flowers, greens, edible cacti, and other wild edible plants you have foraged. This chapter includes easy recipes with detailed instructions on how to cook healthy meals for yourself and your family.

Prepare tasty dishes using mushrooms and other wild edible plants you have foraged. [67]

## Cooking Tips

Follow these cooking tips before preparing your recipes.

- Read the ingredients list and instructions before cooking
- Experiment with different wild edible plants and ingredients while cooking
- Season and taste while preparing the recipe
- Pay attention to the food texture
- Don't experiment with ingredients or improvise when baking
- Use simple recipes that highlight the wild plant's flavors
- Taste the plant before using it to ensure that the texture and flavor meet your expectations
- Preserve any wild plants you won't use to increase their lifespan
- Use different cooking methods like grilling, roasting, and sauteing
- Wear gloves when cleaning cactus pads to protect your hands from the thorns

Are you ready to discover new recipes and start cooking?

# Prickly Pear Cactus Pad Tacos with Sautéed Vegetables and Avocado Crema

The prickly pear cactus pad isn't your typical taco. This Mexican dish has a special flavor and aroma that will make you feel like you're eating at a Mexican restaurant. The avocado cream on top gives it a mouthwatering taste.

### Ingredients:

- 4-6 fresh cactus pads
- Juice of two limes
- 6 large, diced tomatoes
- 1 garlic clove
- ½ diced onion
- Salt and pepper to taste
- 1 package of corn or flour tortilla

Use thinly sliced mushrooms to cook this meal. "

- 1 round of fresh goat cheese

**Sauteed Vegetables Ingredients:**

- 5-6 thinly sliced mushrooms
- 1-2 sliced bell peppers
- 1 chopped zucchini
- 1 sliced jalapeno
- 1 sliced onion
- 3-4 diced cloves garlic
- ⅓ cup of cilantro
- 1 tablespoon of oregano
- 1 tablespoon of cumin
- 1-2 tablespoons of olive oil
- ½ tablespoon of cayenne pepper (optional)

**Avocado Cream Ingredients:**

- 1 medium avocado
- ¼ teaspoon of garlic powder
- ¼ teaspoon of ground cumin
- 1 tablespoon of lime juice
- 2 tablespoons of mayonnaise
- ½ cup of sour cream or Greek yogurt
- ½ teaspoon of salt

**Cleaning the Cactus Pads Instructions:**

1. Clean the cactus pads by putting them on a cutting board and cutting off the edges with a sharp knife.
2. Remove the thorns and spines from the front and the back with a knife.
3. Wash the cutting board.
4. Rinse the cactus pads with water and then put them back on the cutting board to start cooking.

## Cooking Prickly Pear Cactus Pad Tacos Instructions:

1. Cut the cactus pads on a cutting board into vertical strips and then cut them horizontally.
2. Place the cactus pad pieces in a large pot and fill it with water.
3. Add the onion, garlic, tomatoes, and salt.
4. Boil it uncovered on medium heat for ten minutes or until the cactus pad slices feel tender.
5. Lower the heat if the gelatinous sticky substance in the cactus pads starts to foam.
6. Drain the cactus slices and let them cool.
7. Put them in a large bowl until you prepare the rest of the recipe.

## Sauteed Vegetables Instructions:

1. Put one tablespoon of olive oil in a large pan and leave it on medium heat.
2. Add the onions and let them cook for four minutes. They should start to look translucent.
3. Add the zucchini and peppers and cook for five minutes or until the peppers feel tender. Stir occasionally.
4. Add the other tablespoon of olive oil to prevent the vegetables from sticking to the pan.
5. Toss the garlic, mushrooms, cayenne pepper, oregano, and cumin.
6. Cook for three minutes or until the vegetables turn light brown.

## Avocado Crema Instructions:

1. Blend all the ingredients until they are smooth.
2. Place in an airtight container wrapped with plastic and leave it in the refrigerator for eight hours.

## Making the Tacos:

1. Assemble the tacos with the tortillas and goat cheese.
2. Fill the tortillas with the sauteed vegetables and the cooked cactus pads, then put the avocado crema on top.

# Nopalitos (Cactus Pads) and Black Bean Quesadillas

This dish is perfect for vegetarians looking for a tasty snack or a filling dinner. The cactus pads and the quesadillas give this dish a distinctive and flavorful taste.

## Ingredients:

- 1 15-ounce can of black beans
- 10 flour tortillas, 7-inch diameter
- 1 cup of frozen corn
- ½ cup of chopped fresh cilantro
- ½ cup of diced red onion
- 2 cups of shredded cheddar cheese
- 1 minced garlic clove
- 1 batch of taco seasoning

## Instructions:

1. Clean and cook the cactus pads using the instructions above.
2. Drain the black beans and put them in a large bowl.
3. Add the frozen corn.
4. Add the nopalitos, taco seasoning, shredded cheddar, chopped cilantro, minced garlic, and diced onion to the corn and beans.
5. Stir to mix the ingredients.
6. Put half a cup of the filling on each side of the tortilla and fold.
7. Put the quesadillas in a skillet and cook over medium heat until the cheese melts and both sides turn crispy and brown.
8. Cut into triangles and serve.

# Acorn Squash Soup with Toasted Mesquite Seeds

Enjoy this creamy soup on a cold winter night, and savor the acorn flavor with the mesquite seeds.

Use 2 tablespoons of mesquite seeds for this recipe. [69]

## Ingredients:

- 2 tablespoons of mesquite seeds
- 2 medium acorn squash
- 2 tablespoons of fresh lemon juice
- 3 unpeeled garlic cloves
- 4 cups of vegetable broth
- 2 tablespoons of extra-virgin olive oil-
- 1 tablespoon of extra-virgin olive oil for drizzling
- ⅛ teaspoon of cayenne pepper
- 1 large yellow chopped onion
- ¼ teaspoon of nutmeg
- 2 medium chopped carrots
- 1 tablespoon of fresh thyme leaves
- 1 tablespoon of fresh thyme leaves for garnish
- 1 teaspoon sea salt
- 1 teaspoon sea salt for sprinkling

## Toasting the Mesquite Seeds Ingredients:

- 1 tablespoon of olive oil
- Dash of salt and pepper

## Instructions:

1. Preheat the oven to 400 °F.
2. Place parchment paper on a baking sheet.
3. Cut the acorn squash in half and then remove the seeds.
4. Drizzle olive oil over the squash halves.
5. Sprinkle the salt and pepper.
6. Put the acorn squash on the baking sheet with the cut side down.
7. Place the garlic cloves in a piece of foil.
8. Add a pinch of salt and a drizzle of oil, and then wrap the foil paper.
9. Put them on the baking sheet.
10. Roast for 45 minutes or until the acorn squash feels tender.
11. Remove the baking sheet from the oven and let it cool down.
12. Peel the foil wrap and discard it.
13. Remove the squash flesh to fill 2 ½ cups and save the remaining flesh for later.
14. Discard the squash skin.
15. Place the olive oil in a large pot and heat over medium heat.
16. Add the salt, carrots, and onion, and cook for eight minutes or until the vegetables feel tender. Stir occasionally.
17. Add the pepper grinds, cayenne, and nutmeg, and stir.
18. Add the 2 ½ cups of roasted squash, thyme leaves, broth, and garlic, and stir.
19. Simmer for 20 minutes.
20. Let the soup cool down, then blend it with lemon juice until smooth.
21. Clean and dry the mesquite seeds.
22. Toast the seeds by mixing them with a dash of salt and pepper and olive oil.
23. Preheat the oven to 325 °F and bake the seeds for 20 minutes.

24. Place on top of the soup.

25. Season to taste.

26. Put into bowls, drizzle with olive oil, and add a tablespoon of fresh thyme leaves for garnish.

# Desert Hackberry Jam

Who doesn't love jam? This delicious recipe is easy to prepare and is the perfect topping for your favorite dessert. You can also have it with butter toast for breakfast.

### Ingredients:

- 4 cups of desert hackberries
- 4 tablespoons of pectin
- 4 tablespoons of lemon juice
- 4 cups of granulated sugar
- 1 teaspoon of butter

### Instructions:

1. Remove pests, leaves, stems, and unripe berries.

2. Clean the hackberries by rinsing them with water.

3. Put the hackberries in a saucepan.

4. Add the sugar, lemon juice, and zest to the saucepan.

5. Simmer over medium heat for 15 minutes.

6. Whisk in with pectin until it dissolves.

7. Boil the mixture over medium-high heat for two minutes.

8. Add one teaspoon of butter.

9. Use a ladle to place the jam into sterilized mason jars and leave ½ inch of headspace.

10. Wipe the jars' rims with a paper towel.

11. Seal tight with lids.

12. Fill a canner with hot water and then add the jars. The water should cover the jars.

13. Boil the water to process the jam over medium-high heat for ten minutes.

# Prickly Pear Cactus Fruit Sorbet

Cool down with this sugary sorbet on a hot summer day. It is the perfect dessert to serve to friends or children.

Prickly pear cactus fruit. [70]

## Ingredients:

- 9 large prickly pear cactus fruits
- 1 lemon juiced
- ½ cup of agave syrup

## Instructions:

1. Put on gloves and clean the cactus or burn off the thorns with a gas burner or a grill.
2. Let the cactus cool.
3. Wear an apron to protect your clothes from staining, and keep the gloves on.
4. Peel the fruits and discard the spines, peels, and tough ends.
5. Blend the fruits in a juicer or food processor.
6. Remove the seeds with a mesh sieve.
7. Add the lemon juice and syrup. You may need less syrup, so add a few drops, then taste.
8. Pour the mixture into a baking dish and leave it in the freezer.
9. Remove from the freezer every 30 minutes and rake with a fork to form icy crystals.

# Desert Marigold and Indian Paintbrush Salad

This salad is the perfect dinner meal if you want to lose weight or have a healthy snack.

**Ingredients:**

- 1 8-ounce can of undrained mandarin oranges
- Two teaspoons of fresh desert marigold petals
- 1 16-ounce can of crushed and undrained pineapples
- 6 cups of combined fresh and sliced fruits of your choice
- 1 5-ounce package of instant lemon pudding mix
- 2 bananas
- 1 large container of Cool Whip
- 1 bag of chopped nuts
- ½ bag of miniature marshmallows

**Instructions:**

1. Put the pudding mix in a large bowl.
2. Add the six cups of fresh fruits, Cool Whip, nuts, marshmallows, oranges, and pineapples to the large bowl (Leave some of the Cool Whip for garnish).
3. Cover the salad bowl and let it chill overnight.
4. Peel and cut the bananas into small slices and add to the mixture.
5. Add the fresh marigold petals and toss.
6. Garnish with the remaining Cool Whip and serve.

# Purslane and Miner's Lettuce Salad

This healthy and delicious salad is suitable for any meal and can also be served as a light dinner.

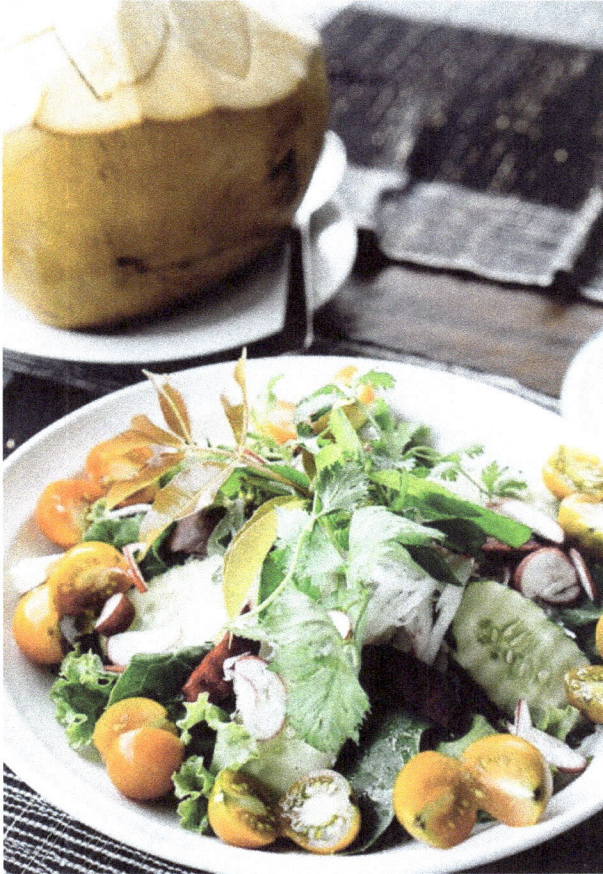

Purslane and miner's lettuce salad. [71]

## Ingredients:

- 3 cups of chopped miner's lettuce
- 3 cups of chopped Purslane
- 1 cup of chopped fresh mint
- 1 cup of diced cucumbers
- 1 cup of diced tomatoes
- Salt and pepper for seasoning

**Dressing Ingredients:**

- ¼ cup of olive oil
- ½ teaspoon of salt
- 2 teaspoons of ground sumac
- ½ teaspoon of minced garlic
- ¼ cup of fresh lemon juice

**Instructions:**

1. Rinse the Purslane with water and chop the leaves, stems, and roots, then wash again.
2. Let it dry in the salad spinner.
3. Remove the mint leaves from the stems and dry in the salad spinner.
4. Chop the mint leaves.
5. Chop the miner's lettuce, rinse, and dry in the salad spinner.
6. Peel and cut the cucumbers into small slices.
7. Chop the tomatoes.
8. Mix the salt, sumac, garlic, and lemon juice in a small bowl.
9. Add one tablespoon of olive oil at a time and whisk until the dressing is well-blended.
10. Place the salad ingredients in a large bowl, then drizzle the dressing.
11. Season with salt and pepper to taste.
12. Garnish with sumac.
13. You can eat it fresh or leave it overnight in the fridge.

# Morchella Mushroom and Wild Rice Stuffed Bell Peppers

If you want to try a new dish, this is the recipe for you. It is comforting and tasty, thanks to the combination of mushrooms, rice, and peppers that will keep you satisfied and full.

**Ingredients:**

- 8 ounces of Morchella mushrooms
- 4 bell peppers, any color

- 1 cup of wild rice
- ¼ cup of chopped fresh parsley
- 2 minced garlic cloves
- 1 chopped onion
- 1 tablespoon of olive oil
- ½ teaspoon of salt
- 2 cups of water
- Salt and pepper to taste
- ½ cup of shredded cheese (optional)

**Instructions:**

1. Preheat the oven to 375 °F.
2. Chop off the peppers' tops and remove the membranes and seeds.
3. Rinse the rice in cold water and let it drain.
4. Put the salt and water in a medium saucepan and let it boil.
5. Stir in the rice to mix.
6. Lower the heat, cover the saucepan, and let the salt simmer for 45 minutes or until the water is absorbed and the rice feels tender.
7. Put the olive oil in a large skillet and heat over medium heat.
8. Add the garlic and onion and cook until the onion softens.
9. Add the mushrooms and cook until they feel tender.
10. Add the parsley and wild rice and season with salt and pepper.
11. Stuff the bell peppers with the mushroom mixture and wild rice.
12. Put the stuffed peppers in a baking dish.
13. Sprinkle shredded cheese over the peppers.
14. Bake in the oven for 30 minutes or until the cheese melts and the peppers feel tender.

# Agaricus Mushroom and Nopalitos Enchiladas

Prepare this exotic dish for a delicious dinner meal for you and your family.

**Ingredients:**

- 2 chopped green onions
- ¼ cup of sliced black olives
- 2 12-ounce jars of Herdez Tomatillo Verde Sauce
- 2 cups of shredded low-fat Monterey Jack cheese
- 8-12 corn tortillas
- 1 teaspoon of red pepper flakes
- ¼ teaspoon of ground black pepper
- 4-5 ounces of white button mushrooms
- ½ 15-ounce jar of Doña Maria nopalitos
- 2 garlic cloves peeled and minced
- 1 medium-sliced white onion
- 2 tablespoons of canola oil

**Instructions:**

1. Preheat the oven to 175 °F.
2. Coat a nine-inch rectangular baking dish with canola cooking spray.
3. Put the olive oil in a large frying pan and heat over medium-high.
4. Add the onions and sauté for three minutes.
5. Add the nopalitos, mushrooms, and garlic.
6. Sauté the vegetables for five minutes or until the mushrooms feel soft.
7. Season with black pepper and red pepper flakes.
8. Add ¼ cup of the Herdez Tomatillo Verde Sauce to the mushrooms mixture.
9. Put ½ cup of the Herdez Tomatillo Verde Sauce in a small frying pan and warm it over medium heat.
10. Dip one corn tortilla in the sauce.
11. Put two tablespoons of the vegetable mixture and nopalitos in the tortilla.

12. Sprinkle one tablespoon of shredded cheese on top.

13. Roll the tortilla and put it on the baking sheet.

14. Repeat the previous steps until you finish all the tortillas.

15. Pour the remaining Tomatillo Verde Sauce over the tortillas.

16. Sprinkle more cheese.

17. Bake in the preheated oven for ten minutes.

18. Let it sit for ten minutes.

19. Garnish with green onions.

# Morel Mushroom Pizza with Sausage and Green Garlic

Everyone loves pizza. It is delicious and cheesy and allows you to experiment with different ingredients. This recipe highlights the morel mushrooms' tasty flavor, giving the pizza an amazing taste.

Morel mushroom pizza with sausage and green garlic. [73]

## Ingredients:

- 8 ounces of chopped morel mushrooms
- 2 hot Italian sausages with casings removed
- 1 ball of pizza dough
- 2 tablespoons of olive oil
- ¼ cup of cornmeal
- 4 ounces of grated parmesan or sharp cheddar
- 4 ounces of goat cheese
- 1 teaspoon of dried thyme
- A handful of fresh arugula
- ½ teaspoon of crushed red pepper flakes
- 4 stalks of sliced green garlic
- Extra virgin olive oil
- Salt and pepper to taste
- Sea salt for serving

## Instructions:

1. Preheat the oven to 475 °F.
2. Place a baking sheet in the oven until you are ready to start baking.
3. Put one tablespoon of olive oil in a large iron skillet and leave it over medium heat.
4. Add the sausages and let them cook for five minutes or until the meat turns light brown.
5. Use a wooden spoon to break up the meat.
6. Remove the sausages from the skillet with a slotted spoon and place them on a paper towel to drain.
7. Add the garlic to the pan and stir.
8. Let it cook for three minutes or until the garlic feels soft.
9. Remove the garlic from the pan with tongs and put it in a small bowl.
10. Put one tablespoon of olive oil in the pan, then add the salt, pepper, thyme, red pepper flakes, and mushrooms.

11. Stir and let them cook for eight minutes or until the ingredients turn tender or light brown.
12. Remove the pan from the stove and add the sausages to the mixture.
13. Spread the dough on a flat surface with cornmeal scattered on the surface.
14. Brush oil onto the dough's surface, then add the sausage and mushroom mixture all over the dough.
15. Scatter the cheese on the dough, and then gently add the crust.
16. Bake the pizza in the preheated oven until the edges turn crisp and brown.
17. Put the arugula in a small bowl, add olive oil, and mix.
18. Remove the pizza from the oven and add the arugula while it is still hot.
19. Sprinkle sea salt, slice, and serve before it gets cold.

# Indian Potato Curry

Enjoy this Indian potato recipe with the mouthwatering curry flavor. This dish is perfect for a light lunch or dinner.

Indian potato curry. [78]

## Ingredients:

- 2 medium potatoes
- 5-6 curry leaves or cilantro
- 1 teaspoon of coriander powder
- ½ teaspoon of turmeric powder
- ½ teaspoon of red chili powder
- 1 teaspoon of garlic paste
- 1 teaspoon of ginger paste
- ½ teaspoon of nigella seeds (also called onion seeds)
- ½ teaspoon of cumin seeds
- ½ teaspoon of mustard seeds
- ¼ cup of cooking oil
- 1 teaspoon of tamarind paste or mango powder
- 1 green chili
- 1 teaspoon of salt
- 1 teaspoon of sugar

## Instructions:

1. Put the potatoes in an instant pot and let them boil until they soften.
2. Peel the potatoes and cut them into quarters.
3. Press each quarter with your hand and break it into chunks.
4. Put the oil in a wok or a stir-frying pan and leave it on medium heat.
5. Add the nigella seeds, cumin, and mustard to the oil and let them heat for 30 seconds.
6. Add the garlic paste, ginger, and powdered spices.
7. Let them sauté for a minute.
8. Add the potatoes to the mixture and combine.
9. Add two cups of water, salt, sugar, tamarind paste, green chili, and curry leaves.
10. Cook uncovered for ten minutes.
11. Serve with bread.

# Fried Puffball Mushrooms

The puffball mushrooms are delicious and are a great addition to any dish. You can also fry them and enjoy their taste as the main ingredient.

**Ingredients:**

- 8 ounces of fresh puffball mushrooms
- Grapeseed oil
- 3 large beaten eggs
- panko breadcrumbs
- 1.5 cups of all-purpose flour
- ½ teaspoon of black pepper
- 1.5 teaspoons of salt
- Extra virgin olive oil (for dressing)
- Fresh lemon juice (for dressing)
- Fresh arugula (for dressing)

**Instructions:**

1. Preheat the oven to 225 °F.
2. Put the flour in a large bowl, then add the salt and mix.
3. Cut the mushrooms' root ends.
4. Check the mushrooms for damage. The meat should be white – not yellow or green.
5. Cut the mushroom into half-inch pieces with a sharp knife.
6. Coat the mushroom pieces in flour, dip them in the beaten eggs, and then in the panko breadcrumbs.
7. Heat half a cup of grapeseed oil in a pan on medium heat.
8. Add the mushroom pieces after the oil is heated.
9. Fry each side until they turn golden brown.
10. Make sure that the mushrooms don't get burned, and lower the heat if necessary.
11. The oil should cover the breadcrumbs, and the pan shouldn't get dry. If it does, add more oil.

12. After the mushrooms turn brown, put the pan in the preheated oven on a cookie sheet with a resting rack so the heat doesn't get trapped.

13. After the mushrooms are fried, remove the pan from the oven and sprinkle them with salt.

14. Add the olive oil, lemon juice, and arugula for the dressing.

15. Season with salt and pepper to taste and serve hot.

# Wild Onion Pasta

This tasty pasta is unlike anything you have tried before. The wild onion gives it a unique and strong flavor.

Wild onions. [74]

### Ingredients:

- 1 pound of wild onions
- 2 tablespoons of grated Parmigiano Reggiano
- 3 tablespoons of unsalted butter
- 8 ounces of dried spaghetti
- 1 peeled and minced garlic clove
- Salt and pepper

**Instructions:**

1. Rinse the wild onions and trim them to match the spaghetti's length.
2. Fill a pan with water, season with salt and pepper, and boil.
3. Put two tablespoons of butter in a frying pan and heat over medium heat.
4. Add the garlic and then the onions when the butter starts bubbling.
5. Add the spaghetti to the boiling water and cook according to the pack's instructions.
6. While the pasta cooks, stir the onions for five minutes or until they wilt.
7. Add one or two ladles of pasta water to the onions until they soften.
8. Once the spaghetti is cooked, add it to the onions with one ladle of water.
9. Add one tablespoon of butter and season with salt and pepper.
10. Sprinkle two tablespoons of Parmigiano Reggiano, stir, and serve.

# Garlic Mashed Yucca

This creamy side dish goes with any meal. You will enjoy it so much that you will eat it by itself.

**Ingredients:**

- 2 pounds of rinsed, peeled, and chopped yucca root
- 3 large, smashed cloves of garlic
- 1-2 tablespoons of butter
- 1 tablespoon of butter for serving
- ½ teaspoon of black pepper
- ½ teaspoon of salt
- ½ teaspoon of salt for serving
- 4-5 cups of chicken, bone, or vegetable broth
- 1 cup of broth for mashing
- Microgreens for garnish

**Instructions:**

1. Cut the yucca roots into chunks and remove the outer skin, leaving the white flesh.
2. Slice the white flesh into one-inch pieces.
3. Put the yucca in a large pot and cover it with one inch of broth.
4. Add the salt and smashed garlic.
5. Boil the mixture over high heat.
6. Reduce the heat, cover, and let the mixture simmer for 25 minutes or until the yucca feels tender.
7. Drain the mixture and put it in a large bowl.
8. Add the pepper and butter to the yucca and beat with a stand mixer until they turn fluffy and creamy.
9. Pour the extra broth over the mixture a little at a time to achieve the desired creamy texture.
10. Season with salt to taste and put in a serving bowl.
11. Garnish with the microgreens and serve.

# Southern Wild Onion Pie

This Southern delicacy with subtle nuances of wild onions is the perfect dinner dish for you and your family.

Southern wild onion pie. [75]

## Ingredients:

- 2 to 4 pounds of thinly sliced wild onions
- 3 tablespoons of fresh chopped chives
- ¾ cup of mayonnaise
- 1 ¼ cups of grated parmesan
- 1 pie shell
- 3 cups of caramelized onions
- Salt and pepper
- 2 eggs
- 4 dashes of hot pepper sauce
- ¾ cup of Greek yogurt
- 3 tablespoons of cooking sherry
- Salt and pepper to taste

## Instructions:

1. Put the sliced onions in a slow cooker.
2. Cook on high for five hours until the onions are softened and turn golden brown.
3. After the onions are cooked, put them in a large bowl and let them cool.
4. Preheat the oven to 375 °F.
5. Mix three cups of the cooked onions with yogurt in a large bowl.
6. Add salt, pepper, eggs, and hot sauce.
7. Mix them, then add the pie shell.
8. Mix the salt, pepper, mayonnaise, and grated cheese in a small bowl until they are fully blended.
9. Cover the crust in aluminum foil to protect it from burning.
10. Let it bake for 35 minutes in the oven.
11. Remove the foil, then let it bake for an extra 15 minutes or until the top turns golden brown.
12. Garnish with chives.
13. Let the pie cool down for a few minutes, then slice and serve.

# Wolfberry Leaves and Seeds Soup

This soup is high in nutrients and will boost your immunity. It is perfect for when you are sick and need to increase your energy.

**Ingredients:**

- 1 bundle of wolfberry leaves
- 5 slices of ginger
- 2 slices of pork liver
- 1 tablespoon of wolfberry seeds
- 1 egg
- Salt for seasoning

**Instructions:**

1. Fill a bowl with water, add salt, and soak the wolfberry leaves for 15 minutes.
2. Rinse the leaves with water.
3. Fill a large cooking pot with ten glasses of water and boil on high heat for five minutes.
4. Add the wolfberry seeds and liver slices.
5. Let them boil until the liver slices are half-cooked.
6. Add the wolfberry leaves, but don't overcook them.
7. Season with salt, then whisk the egg and add it slowly to the soup.
8. Cover and let it simmer for 15 minutes or less (Check every few minutes and remove when it meets your desired texture).
9. Serve hot.

If you aren't an experienced cook, make sure to follow the recipes with the exact ingredients and instructions. Later, you can experiment with different ingredients and get creative.

# Chapter 7: Medicinal Plants of the Southwest

Administering medicinal plants and herbs seems like a mythical practice based only on belief. However, did you know that the healing properties of many plants have been scientifically proven? In fact, quite a few modern medicines are synthesized from medicinal plants.

Practice making your own medicinal plants. [76]

Think about it – how are certain plants not infected with diseases even after coming in contact with diseased insects, mammals, and fungi? They create defensive compounds to protect themselves, which humans can use to cure and prevent their diseases.

# The Ancient Roots of Medicinal Plants

Medicinal plants were used before the dawn of civilization. Back in prehistoric times (around 2.5 million years ago), humans settled in areas surrounded by medicinal plants. Growth of useful herbs was also found around their burial sites, indicating that they may have tried to cure the person using natural remedies before death.

Irrefutable proof of human ancestors using medicinal plants was found on clay tablets dating back to the Sumerian civilization (circa 3,000 BCE, settled in present-day Iraq). The tablets recorded more than 800 natural medicines! Other civilizations in Asia and Europe also kept written records of their discoveries.

However, the ancient Native Americans passed down their knowledge orally, so historians aren't sure when the practice of using plant medicines began in the U.S. It is generally accepted that the native settlers in the Southwest have been practicing it for thousands of years. For Indigenous tribes like the Navajo, Apache, Hopi, and Pueblo, medicinal plants carry a spiritual significance, too.

For instance, sage (salvia officinalis) has been used for their purification rituals and to treat colds, coughs, and digestive issues for several centuries. The Zuni tribe used the leaves of the century plant (Agave americana) to treat wounds and the root to cure digestive problems. Yucca was used for the treatment of arthritis and skin sores, and the prickly pear cactus acted as a natural healer of wounds and burns.

So far, the Native Americans have made their own discoveries regarding medicinal plants without any outside influence. When the Spanish colonized the Americas in the 16th century, they brought their own vast knowledge of plant medicines carefully gathered and recorded since the dawn of civilization. Both the Indigenous peoples and the European settlers learned from each other to greatly advance the discipline.

In the 19th and 20th centuries, scientists began formally studying the medicinal plants of the Southwest. Reputable botanists like Edward Palmer and John Muir heavily documented the traditional uses of these plants. Echinacea angustifolia, a purple cone-shaped flower, was long known for its immune-boosting properties. Chaparral was used traditionally to treat a variety of ailments, including inflammation and infections. Ephedra viridis tea is stimulating and historically used to treat respiratory issues.

Today, many of these plants are still used in both traditional and modern herbal medicine. There is a growing interest in holistic and natural remedies, and the medicinal plants of the Southwest continue to be studied for their therapeutic potential. You can test their potential yourself when you find many of these natural healing plants during your foraging endeavors.

# Common Medicinal Plants of the Southwest

Did you know that over 50,000 species of plants are used for medicinal purposes? The Southwest is home to many of those species, discovered and extensively used by the Native Americans. Some species are preferred over others, not just because they are more effective but also because they are easily available.

### Yucca (Yucca spp.)

You may know Yucca better by the names Spanish Dagger, Adam's Needle, or Soapweed, depending on the specific species. It is a perennial (available in all seasons) plant belonging to the family Asparagaceae, widely found throughout the Southwest. It has tough, sword-like leaves and tall, flowering stalks that bear clusters of white or cream-colored flowers. The plant thrives in arid and semi-arid regions and is well-adapted to desert environments.

- **Therapeutic Properties:** Yucca contains saponins and polyphenolics, which are known to reduce inflammation, thus helping manage the symptoms of arthritis. The plant is overflowing with antioxidants, protecting your cells from oxidative stress. Certain compounds in yucca prevent the growth of bacteria and fungi, which can make your body immune to harmful microbes. It is also known to alleviate symptoms of gastrointestinal disorders.

- **Traditional Uses:** Native American tribes have traditionally used yucca root to treat arthritis and joint pain. The root is usually prepared as a tea. Its extracts have been applied to the body to treat skin conditions such as sores, wounds, and infections. A decoction (boiled plant) of yucca root has been used for a long time to soothe digestive disorders. The saponins in yucca create a natural lather, so it is utilized as a soap and hair conditioner.

- **Preparation and Usage:** Yucca is most commonly consumed as a tea or a decoction, but you can also make a paste from the root to treat skin conditions and wounds. To use it as a shampoo, simply crush the plant and mix it in water.

After foraging yucca, don't use it as a medicine before consulting your health advisor, especially if you're pregnant, since it affects the digestive system.

### Prickly Pear Cactus (Opuntia spp.)

Prickly pear cactus is also called nopal, nopales, Indian fig, and tuna. It belongs to the Cactaceae family and is found throughout the Southwestern deserts. Unlike most other cacti, the prickly pear has flat, rounded pads (cladodes) covered with spines. Both its pads and fruits (called tunas) are edible.

- **Therapeutic Properties:** Prickly pear produces the betalains compound, which has anti-inflammatory effects. It is abundant in antioxidants like flavonoids, polyphenols, and vitamin C, helping your body fight viruses and bacteria and improve your immune system. It acts as a hypoglycemic, bringing your blood sugar levels and cholesterol under control. If you run out of water while foraging in the desert, you can eat tunas to hydrate yourself since they contain around 85% water.

- **Traditional Uses:** Prickly pear pads are traditionally consumed as part of a meal to control glucose spikes. Their high fiber content also aids in digestion. Its juice or pulp is used to reduce hangovers. Early (and even modern) skincare cosmetics were made from the oil extracted from prickly pear seeds. The oil also heals minor wounds.

- **Preparation and Usage:** Nopales are commonly grilled, boiled, or sautéed and used in salads, tacos, and other dishes. You can dry the pads to make tea for experiencing its anti-inflammatory properties.

Prickly pear is generally safe for consumption and skin applications, but diabetics should monitor their blood sugar level periodically since it can lower it considerably.

## Chaparral (Larrea Tridentata)

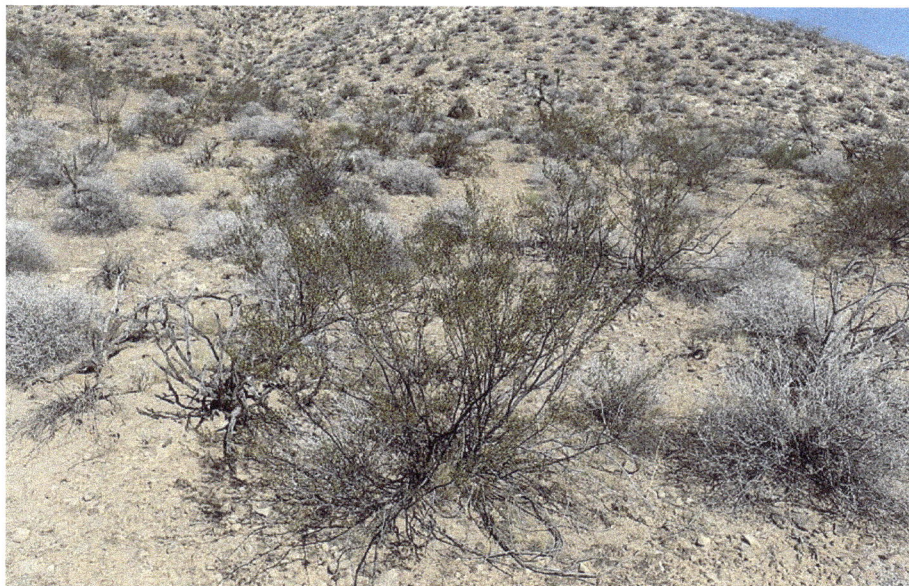

Chaparral. [77]

Commonly known as creosote bush, the chaparral herb hails from the Zygophyllaceae family. It is a hardy shrub that thrives in arid desert environments of the Southwest. It has small, waxy, dark green leaves and yellow flowers, which are followed by fuzzy, white seed pods. The plant emits a distinctive, strong creosote-like odor, especially after rain.

- **Therapeutic Properties:** Chaparral contains nordihydroguaiaretic acid (NDGA), which has potent anti-inflammatory properties and strong antioxidant properties. Apart from being antimicrobial, research suggests that the herb inhibits the growth of certain cancer cells. It's not a downright cure for cancer, but patients can use it as an alternative medicine if the doctor permits. Chaparral is also known to alleviate minor aches and pains.

- **Traditional Uses:** It has been applied to the body to treat wounds, rashes, and insect bites by the Indigenous peoples. They use it as a remedy for colds, coughs, and bronchitis. Chaparral tea or tinctures clear mucus and soothe the respiratory tract. It has also been used to reduce pain and inflammation among arthritis patients. For a long time, it has been used as a blood purifier to support liver health and aid in detoxifying the body.

- **Preparation and Usage:** Chaparral leaves and twigs can be dried and used to make tea to address respiratory issues, digestive health, and detoxification. Alcohol-based extracts of the herb are used for their concentrated therapeutic properties, ideally for inflammation and pain relief. Chaparral salves can be used to treat skin conditions and wounds.

It is crucial to use chaparral under the guidance of a healthcare provider. There have been reports of liver toxicity associated with its use, especially with long-term or high-dose consumption. It is not recommended during pregnancy or breastfeeding.

### Echinacea (Echinacea spp.)

Echinacea, belonging to the family Asteraceae, is more popular as "coneflower" due to the conical shape that its flowers take. Their petals are usually purple, white, or pink, and the cone in the middle is brownish. The plants are perennial and can grow between one and three feet tall.

They have lance-shaped leaves and prefer to grow in wooded areas, prairies, or barrens. You can find them in many parts of the Central and Eastern U.S., and in the Southwest, you can forage for them in grasslands and shrublands.

- **Therapeutic Properties:** Echinacea is widely used to amplify immune function. It is believed to stimulate the production of white blood cells. It has anti-inflammatory and antimicrobial properties, acts as an antioxidant, and aids in wound healing.

- **Traditional Uses:** Native Americans used Echinacea to treat coughs, colds, and sore throats. It also healed skin wounds and relieved toothaches and throat infections. A few tribes were known to use it to treat stomach cramps and indigestion.

- **Preparation and Usage:** Echinacea is primarily consumed as a tea, but it can be added to your skin creams to treat conditions like eczema and psoriasis.

Echinacea is generally safe for short-term use. Potential side effects include gastrointestinal discomfort, allergic reactions (particularly in those allergic to plants in the daisy family), and rash. It is not recommended if you have autoimmune disorders, as it may stimulate the immune system.

### Mullein (Verbascum Thapsus)

Mullein is native to Asia and Europe but thrives in the disturbed areas (like roadsides) of Arizona and Southern California. Its family name is

Scrophulariaceae. It is a biennial plant (completes its life cycle in two years) that forms a rosette of lance-shaped leaves in its first year and a tall, flowering spike in its second year.

Mullein can grow up to 10 feet tall, and its leaves are velvety to the touch (you may mistake them for fake leaves!). Its flowers are small, yellow, and densely packed along the upper part of the flowering spike.

- **Therapeutic Properties:** Mullein is renowned for its ability to soothe the respiratory tract. It is used to treat coughs, bronchitis, asthma, and other respiratory issues. It has anti-inflammatory properties and antimicrobial properties. It acts as an expectorant, helping to loosen and expel mucus from the lungs.

- **Traditional Uses:** Native Americans long ago discovered Mullein's ability to treat colds and coughs. It was also believed to cure tuberculosis. Mullein flower oil has been used to treat ear infections and relieve ear pain. Its leaves were applied to the skin to treat wounds, burns, and other skin conditions. It was also used to treat diarrhea and promote urine production.

- **Preparation and Usage:** Mullein tea is made by steeping the dried leaves and flowers in hot water to treat sore throats and coughs. Its tincture (alcohol mixture) can be used to cure respiratory conditions. Mullein oil, especially when combined with garlic, is used as an earache remedy.

Short-term use of Mullein has produced little to no side effects so far. However, long-term usage is not recommended unless prescribed by your doctor.

### Ocotillo (Fouquieria Splendens)

Ocotillo is one of the most easily recognizable medicinal plants in the Southwest. It belongs to the Fouquieriaceae family and looks like a weathered aquatic coral. It is found in the desert, hence its nickname, desert coral.

It has long, spiny, whip-like stems that can reach up to 20 feet in height. The stems are usually leafless except after rains when they quickly sprout small, green leaves. In spring, the plant produces bright red tubular flowers at the tips of the stems.

- **Therapeutic Properties:** Ocotillo is believed to stimulate the lymphatic system (the delicate tube network in your body), promoting the movement and drainage of lymph fluids. It has anti-inflammatory properties and helps support digestive health. It can also be used to relieve pain and clear accumulated mucus.

- **Traditional Uses:** The Native American tribes of Cahuilla and Pima have been reaping ocotillo's lymphatic benefits for generations. Women especially used it to treat menstrual cramps and regulate their cycles.

- **Preparation and Usage:** You can consume an ocotillo tincture to care for your lymphatic health. Tea can be made from the bark to aid digestion and maintain respiratory health. You can also create a paste to treat skin conditions and wounds.

Ocotillo is safe if taken in small amounts. Large doses can lead to digestive problems. Since it affects digestion, it's not recommended during pregnancy.

## Juniper (Juniperus spp.)

Juniper tree. [78]

Juniper trees and shrubs grow abundantly in the northern part of the world, but you can find them in the Southwest, too. Their family is called Cupressaceae. They start off with needle-like leaves, and as they grow older, their leaves take on a scale-like structure. Female plants produce bluish berry-like cones. You can usually find them in the mountain ranges.

- **Therapeutic Properties:** Juniper berries have strong antiseptic properties, which are ideal for disinfecting wounds. They also have anti-inflammatory, antimicrobial, and digestion-controlling properties.

- **Traditional Uses:** The Indigenous tribes used juniper for cleansing rituals and to protect against evil spirits. It helped them take care of respiratory issues as well. Treating joint pains was also its major function.

- **Preparation and Usage:** Juniper berries can be chewed as they are or made into tea to help with digestive problems. The plant's oil can be extracted for use in aromatherapy for its calming and purifying properties. It can also be applied to cure skin conditions, but make sure to dilute it before using.

A small dosage of juniper and its berries don't cause any problems, but if used in excess, it can lead to kidney damage. It can have stimulating effects on the uterus, so avoid consuming it during pregnancy.

### Palo Verde (Parkinsonia spp.)

Palo verde is a medicinal deciduous tree in the Fabaceae family. It's a desert specialty in the Southwest, known for its unique green bark and yellow flowers. It can grow as tall as 30 feet, but most species are around 20 feet tall. Its leaves are small and divided twice, like in ferns. Check out the tree in spring when it blooms bright yellow flowers, creating a striking visual display.

- **Therapeutic Properties:** Palo verde is antimicrobial and anti-inflammatory and can be used to treat infections and reduce inflammation in the joints. It has astringent properties that can help tighten tissues and reduce bleeding.

- **Traditional Uses:** The bark and leaves of the palo verde were used to make poultices for treating cuts, sores, and other skin wounds. Its seeds are believed to cure diarrhea and stomach cramps. It was also used to treat headaches and body pains.

- **Preparation and Usage:** Palo verde extracts and poultices are applied to the skin to treat wounds, burns, and inflammation. You can drink its tea to improve your digestive system.

The palo verde tree is generally safe for medicinal use, but it can relieve any existing allergies that may become more severe.

## Wild Mint (Mentha Arvensis)

Wild mint (Lamiaceae family) is a perennial herb with square stems, aromatic leaves, and small purple or white flowers. It grows no longer than two feet tall. It has oval-shaped leaves with serrated edges that produce a strong aroma when crushed.

Its flowers are tubular and usually appear in clusters at the leaf axils. You can find them blooming in summer. It grows in a wet environment, along streams, meadows, and ditches.

- **Therapeutic Properties:** The surroundings of wild mint may not be charming, but it's a powerful medicinal herb. It is especially useful in treating indigestion, gas, and bloating. It helps to relieve muscle spasms and cramps, and it has antimicrobial and anti-inflammatory properties. It acts as an analgesic, reducing headaches, toothaches, and other minor pains.

- **Traditional Uses:** The Native Americans have been drinking wild mint tea to care for their digestive health for centuries. Mint leaves were applied to the forehead or made into a poultice to relieve headaches. They were also used to treat minor insect bites and reduce stress during meditation.

- **Preparation and Usage:** Wild mint tea is a good way to benefit from most of its medicinal properties. The extracted oil, due to its strong yet pleasant odor, is used in aromatherapy. You can also apply it to your skin to treat wounds or reduce inflammation. Wild mint is widely used as a flavoring agent in cooking, giving the cuisine a fresh, minty taste.

Stay away from this plant if you are allergic to its minty taste or strong smells. High doses of mint oil can be toxic and should be used with caution.

## Arnica (Arnica spp.)

Thanks to its bright yellow flowers, this is one of the most beautiful medicinal plants in the Southwest. It's no wonder that it belongs to the sunflower family (Asteraceae) of plants. This perennial herb is around one to two feet tall, with slightly hairy leaves that can be oval or heart-shaped. Many species are found in the mountains of Colorado, just near the point where the snow begins and the trees end (alpine zone).

- **Therapeutic Properties:** Arnica is anti-inflammatory and antimicrobial. Its pain-relieving properties can reduce muscle pain and soreness. It can also improve blood circulation, which helps heal bruises and other injuries. It also reduces swelling and fluid retention in injured tissues.

- **Traditional Uses:** Traditionally, arnica was used to relieve the pain of rheumatism and arthritis. In some Indigenous cultures, it was used in hair tonics to stimulate hair growth and treat dandruff. Other than Native Americans, doctors also used it to reduce post-surgery swelling and bruising.

- **Preparation and Usage:** Arnica can be made into a cream or a gel to treat bruises, muscle aches, joint pain, and inflammation. Homeopathic medicines can be synthesized from the plant to treat shock and trauma. Arnica oil can be used for a wholesome massage.

Pure arnica is toxic when ingested and should only be used internally in highly diluted homeopathic preparations. External applications may also cause adverse effects during pregnancy.

Important! If you have pre-existing health problems, always consult a doctor before using any medicinal plant.

# Tips for Responsible Foraging of Medicinal Plants

- Proper identification is doubly important for medicinal plants because using a toxic look-alike may be fatal. Distinctive plants like ocotillo and palo verde are easily recognizable, but venomous plants can be mistaken for most of the other medicinal herbs.

- Avoid trampling plants and disturbing their ecology. Take what you need, but leave enough for other living beings in the region. Did you know that many animals also use these plants to heal their wounds?

- Avoid harvesting reproductive parts if you can. Flowers, seeds, and roots are critical for their species to prosper, which will benefit you in the future. For instance, if you are making medicinal tea, collect only the bark of the plant or leaves.

- If there are other foragers in the area, leave more than enough for them. If there's an Indigenous settlement in the vicinity, respectfully gain their permission before foraging.

- Know when to forage for which parts of the plants. Roots are best collected in the fall, and leaves are most potent in the spring.

- Don't forage in the rain to avoid the risk of flash floods and soil erosion. You will be protecting both the plant life and yourself.

- Replant seeds or cuttings to help sustain the plant population if you can spare the time.

- If you're foraging in disturbed areas for, say, mullein, make sure there is no vehicle traffic and industries around. If there are, the plants may have been infected with pollutants, which can adversely affect your health.

- During your exploration, you may encounter more species of medicinal plants than those mentioned here. The Native Americans in the region may also help expand your knowledge. Since they have been orally spreading their expertise, it will help to have a written record. Carry a notebook and a pen, or record your newfound knowledge on your smartphone.

- Carry all the necessary tools for foraging medicinal plants, like knives, shears, etc. Don't forget your gloves if you are looking for medicinal cacti like the prickly pear.

If you may have noticed, little scientific research supports the profound healing powers of these medicinal plants in the Southwest. Your foraging efforts can help bring their medicinal properties to light, and they can greatly advance research, especially for incurable diseases like cancer (e.g., chaparral). As you deepen your understanding of medicinal plants and their applications, the world will be better for it.

Furthermore, you can learn more about additional varieties of medicinal plants directly from the Indigenous communities in the region. Expand your knowledge and promote a holistic approach to health. Your efforts will eventually bring you closer to the natural world as you gain a deeper insight into the dangers of modern living and wholeheartedly embrace your foraging lifestyle.

# Chapter 8: The Southwest Foraging Lifestyle

As you finish this book, take a moment to recall what you've learned so far. You started with the basics of foraging, and now you've developed a deep love and respect for nature. Foraging is a way of life that brings you closer to the natural world.

Learning to identify edible plants and mushrooms was exciting and new in the beginning. Over time, you've gained the necessary skills and a strong appreciation for the environment. You've explored deserts, forests, and mountains, each housing unique plants and experiences.

Foraging teaches patience and care. "

Foraging teaches patience and care. Each trip into nature is a chance to slow down and pay attention. You learn to see the changes in seasons, understand how plants and animals depend on each other, and realize your role in protecting these places. This awareness makes you want to care for and protect these natural areas.

Living a foraging lifestyle is based on sustainable practices. It helps you live in a way that is good for the Earth. Finding your food locally and in season lowers your impact on the environment, supports different species, and keeps ecosystems healthy. Each meal made from foraged food shows your commitment to living in balance with nature.

Foraging also changes the way you cook and eat. The Southwest has interesting flavors, like wild sumac's tart taste or desert sage's earthy flavor. Foraging encourages you to be creative in the kitchen and try new ingredients. The food you make nourishes both your body and your soul, connecting you to the land and your adventures.

To truly embrace a foraging lifestyle, cultivate a forager's mindset, develop a deeper appreciation for the natural world, and approach foraging as a lifelong learning journey. Observation, curiosity, and respect for the interconnectedness of all living things are fundamental. Pay attention to the details of the environment around you. Be curious about every plant, tree, and mushroom you encounter. Respect the delicate balance of nature and strive to protect it.

There is always something new to learn, new places to explore, and new experiences to enjoy. Share your knowledge and passion with others, creating a community of people who love and protect nature.

Foraging in the Southwest blends a connection with nature, sustainable living, and cooking with wild foods. It changes how you see food and how you live your life. Here's to many more adventures in the wild and the beauty and abundance of nature.

# Implications of Adopting a Foraging Lifestyle

Adopting a foraging lifestyle has broader implications that can positively impact your life and the world around you. Here are the benefits:

### Personal Health

Foraging encourages you to eat fresh, unprocessed foods, which are often more nutritious than store-bought, processed alternatives. Wild foods are full of vitamins, minerals, and antioxidants that can boost your health. Incorporating these natural foods into your diet can improve your overall well-being, increase energy levels, and boost your immune system. The physical activity involved in foraging also promotes fitness and mental health, reducing stress and making you calm and mindful of your actions.

### Environmental Conservation

Foraging creates a deeper connection with local ecosystems and a greater environmental appreciation, which leads to more sustainable living practices. When you forage, you learn about the delicate balance of nature and the necessity of preserving habitats. This knowledge encourages you to protect natural areas and practice sustainable harvesting, ensuring that wild plants and animals can thrive. Reducing your reliance on industrial agriculture and processed foods decreases pollution, habitat destruction, and the carbon footprint associated with food production and transportation.

### Community Engagement

Foraging can unite people, giving everyone a shared purpose. These connections strengthen community bonds and collective efforts to protect and restore local ecosystems. Foraging is also an excellent way for intergenerational learning, as you can share traditional knowledge and skills with younger generations, developing continuity and respect for nature.

### Reduced Reliance on Processed Foods

When you adopt a foraging lifestyle, you naturally reduce your dependence on processed and packaged foods. This shift enables you to cook a cleaner diet, free from artificial additives, preservatives, and excessive sugars and salts. Sourcing your food directly from nature gives a clearer understanding of where your food comes from and the effort involved in obtaining it. This awareness strengthens mindful eating habits and a greater appreciation for the value of food.

### Connection with Local Ecosystems

Foraging requires observing and learning about the plants, animals, and landscapes around you. This deeper understanding of local ecosystems helps you develop a sense of place and belonging. You become more attuned to the seasonal changes and the natural cycles that sustain life. This connection enriches your foraging experience and creates a lifelong commitment to environmental stewardship and sustainability.

Adopting a foraging lifestyle promotes a more sustainable and fulfilling way of life. It encourages slowing down, appreciating the natural world, and living in harmony with your surroundings. This holistic approach to living can bring you joy, fulfillment, and a deeper purpose as you contribute to the well-being of yourself, your community, and the planet.

## Continue Your Foraging Journey

The knowledge and skills you've gained here are the foundation for a lifelong adventure filled with exploration, learning, and a deeper connection to the natural world. Here are some ways you can continue to grow and enrich your foraging experience:

### Attend Workshops and Classes

Consider attending workshops and classes to further your foraging knowledge. Many communities offer programs from experienced foragers who can teach you advanced identification skills, sustainable harvesting techniques, and culinary uses for wild plants and mushrooms. These learning opportunities can expand your expertise and introduce you to new and exciting foraging possibilities.

### Join Foraging Groups

Joining local foraging groups can provide you with a supportive community of like-minded individuals. These groups often organize foraging trips, share resources, and offer a platform for exchanging tips and experiences. Being part of a community can enhance your skills, provide encouragement, and allow you to make friends with others who share your passion for nature.

### Spend More Time in Nature

Make a habit of spending more time outdoors, observing and exploring different environments. Regularly visiting forests, meadows, and wetlands will improve your plant and mushroom identification skills. Pay attention to the changes in seasons and how they affect the availability of different wild foods. The more time you spend in nature, the more attuned you will become to its transitions and the available wild edibles.

### Read and Research

Expand your knowledge by reading more books, articles, and research papers on foraging and related topics. Countless resources are available on foraging specific plants, foraging in different regions, and the ecological aspects of wild food harvesting. Staying informed and curious will keep you engaged and motivated in your foraging experiences.

Expand your knowledge by reading more books, articles, and research papers on foraging. [80]

## Practice Sustainable Foraging

Always practice sustainable foraging to ensure that wild food sources remain plentiful for future generations. Harvest responsibly by taking only what you need, leaving enough for wildlife, and ensuring the plants can regenerate. Respect the ecosystems you forage in, and be mindful of your environmental impact.

### Share Your Knowledge

Teach others about the benefits and joys of foraging. Whether through informal gatherings, social media, or community workshops, sharing your knowledge can inspire others to connect with nature and embrace sustainable living. Educating others contributes to a growing community of environmentally conscious foragers.

### Keep a Foraging Journal

Start a foraging journal to document your experiences, discoveries, and lessons learned. Note the locations, seasons, and conditions where you find different plants and mushrooms. Recording observations can deepen your understanding and provide a valuable reference for future foraging trips.

Whether attending workshops, joining foraging groups, or simply spending more time in nature, there are endless ways to expand your foraging horizons. Enjoy the journey, stay curious, and nurture your bond with the environment.

# Integrating Foraged Foods into Everyday Southwestern Life

Incorporating foraged foods into your daily life can be a rewarding and enriching experience. The diverse ingredients of the Southwest can transform your meals and deepen your connection to the natural world. Here are some practical tips to help you integrate foraged foods into your everyday routine:

### Daily Meal Integration

### Start Simple

Begin by adding foraged ingredients to familiar dishes. For example, toss wild greens like dandelion or lamb's quarters into salads, stir-fries, or soups. Replace store-bought herbs with wild ones such as sage, rosemary, or thyme to augment the flavors of your meals.

### Experiment with Wild Fruits

Add wild fruits like prickly pears, juniper berries, and elderberries to your diet. Use them to make jams, jellies, and sauces, or add them to baked goods, smoothies, and desserts. Wild fruits can also be used to infuse water or teas for a refreshing drink.

### Embrace Edible Flowers

Many wildflowers are not only beautiful but also edible. Add colorful blooms like yucca, nasturtium, or marigold to salads, desserts, and beverages for a pop of color and unique flavor.

### Preserving Seasonal Harvests

### Drying

Dry herbs, fruits, and mushrooms to preserve their flavors for future use. Hang herbs in bundles or use a dehydrator to dry fruits and mushrooms. Store them in airtight containers in a cool, dark place. Dried ingredients can be rehydrated and used in soups, stews, teas, and spice blends.

### Freezing

To extend their shelf life, freeze foraged berries, fruits, and greens. Spread them on a baking sheet to freeze individually before transferring them to freezer bags or containers. Frozen foraged foods can be used in smoothies, baked goods, and cooked dishes.

## Canning and Pickling

Preserve your harvest by canning fruits, vegetables, and herbs. Make jams, jellies, and pickles to enjoy the season's flavors year-round. Pickled wild vegetables and fruits add a tangy twist to salads, sandwiches, and charcuterie boards.

## Infusing

Wild herbs and berries can be used to create infused oils, vinegar, and spirits. These infusions can be used in cooking, salad dressings, and cocktails. For example, infuse olive oil with wild sage or rosemary or make juniper berry gin.

You will be reading about these preservation methods in detail in the upcoming section.

## Creativity and Experimentation in the Kitchen

### Try New Recipes

Explore new recipes that highlight foraged ingredients. Look for traditional Southwestern dishes and modern recipes that incorporate wild foods. Experiment with making prickly pear syrup, mesquite flour pancakes, or wild herb pesto.

### Substitute and Enhance

Use foraged ingredients as substitutes or enhancements in your favorite recipes. Swap store-bought greens for wild ones in a quiche, or add wild berries to a fruit tart. This not only adds unique flavors but also increases the nutritional value of your meals.

### Wild Food Pairings

Pair foraged foods with complementary ingredients to create balanced and flavorful dishes. For example, combine the earthy taste of wild mushrooms with garlic and onions in a sauté, or mix the tartness of wild berries with honey and yogurt.

### Preserve the Harvest Together

Get your family or friends involved in the preservation process. Making jams, drying herbs, or pickling vegetables can be fun group activities that teach valuable skills and create lasting memories.

# Preserving and Storing Foraged Foods for Long-Term Enjoyment

Preserving foraged foods allows you to enjoy the flavors and nutritional benefits of wild ingredients year-round. Here are some effective methods to preserve and store your foraged foods:

## Drying

Drying is a simple and effective way to preserve herbs, fruits, and mushrooms.

Use a dehydrator to dry your foraging goods. [81]

### Herbs

**Air Drying:** Gather small bundles of herbs like sage, rosemary, or thyme. Tie the stems together with a string and hang them upside down in a dry, well-ventilated area away from direct sunlight.

**Dehydrator:** Place herbs in a single layer on dehydrator trays. Dry at low temperatures (95 to 115 °F) until they are crisp.

**Storage:** Once dry, crumble the leaves and store them in airtight containers away from light and heat.

### Fruits and Mushrooms

**Air Drying:** Slice fruits and mushrooms thinly and place them on a rack or screen in a well-ventilated area.

**Dehydrator:** Arrange slices on dehydrator trays. Dry at 135 to 145 °F until completely dry and leathery.

**Storage:** Store dried fruits and mushrooms in airtight containers in a cool, dark place.

### Freezing

Freezing is great for preserving berries, fruits, and greens.

### Berries and Fruits

**Preparation:** Wash and dry the fruits thoroughly. Remove stems and pits if necessary.

**Freezing:** Spread the fruits in a single layer on a baking sheet and freeze until solid. Transfer to freezer bags or containers.

**Storage:** Label them with the date and keep them in the freezer for up to a year.

### Greens

**Blanching:** Briefly blanch greens like dandelion or lamb's quarters in boiling water for 1 to 2 minutes, then cool in ice water.

**Freezing:** Drain and pat dry. Spread on a baking sheet to freeze, then transfer to freezer bags or containers.

**Storage:** Label them with the date and store them in the freezer for up to a year.

### Pickling

Pickling is a method to preserve (and often intensify) the flavors of wild vegetables and fruits.

### Basic Pickling Process

**Preparation:** Wash and cut vegetables or fruits into desired shapes.

**Brine:** Prepare a brine with vinegar, water, salt, and spices. The common ratio is 1 part vinegar to 1 part water.

**Pickling:** Pack the vegetables or fruits into sterilized jars, pour the hot brine over them, and seal them.

**Processing:** To ensure a good seal, process the jars in a boiling water bath for 10 to 15 minutes.

**Storage:** Store in a cool, dark place. Allow pickles to mature for at least a few weeks before eating.

### Making Preserves

Preserves, jams, and jellies are excellent ways to enjoy wild fruits throughout the year.

### Basic Jam Recipe

**Preparation:** Wash and chop fruits like prickly pears or elderberries.

**Cooking:** Combine fruit, sugar, and a bit of lemon juice in a large pot. Cook over medium heat, stirring often until thickened.

**Jarring:** Pour the hot mixture into sterilized jars, leaving a small headspace.

**Processing:** Process the jars in a boiling water bath for 10 minutes.

**Storage:** Store in a cool, dark place for up to a year.

### Making Tinctures

Tinctures are concentrated herbal extracts that are easy to make and store.

### Basic Tincture Recipe

**Preparation:** Fill a jar with chopped fresh herbs (such as wild mint) or dried herbs.

**Alcohol:** Pour high-proof alcohol (like vodka) over the herbs until completely covered.

**Steeping:** Seal the jar and let it sit in a cool, dark place for 4 to 6 weeks, shaking it occasionally.

**Straining:** Strain the liquid into a clean jar through a fine mesh sieve or cheesecloth.

**Storage:** Store the tincture in a dark glass bottle, labeling it with the date and contents. When stored properly, tinctures can last for several years.

By using these techniques, you can enjoy the flavors and benefits of foraged foods long after the harvesting season has ended. Whether you dry, freeze, pickle, or make preserves and tinctures, each method helps you savor the essence of the wild throughout the year.

# Culture of Collaboration in Foraging

Sharing knowledge and experiences with others is necessary for fostering an energetic and robust foraging community. Teaching friends and family about foraging and participating in community events and initiatives are excellent ways to spread the benefits and necessity of foraging in this fast-paced world.

## Building Community

Participating in community events and initiatives centered around foraging creates opportunities for people to come together, share stories, and learn from one another. Whether it's through foraging workshops, guided nature walks, or community gardens, these gatherings create belonging and camaraderie among like-minded individuals who share a passion for the outdoors and sustainable living.

## Preserving Traditional Knowledge

Sharing traditional knowledge about foraging ensures that valuable skills and practices are passed down from generation to generation. By teaching younger family members and community members about the plants, mushrooms, and food preservation techniques used by the ancestors, you can help preserve cultural heritage and promote a deeper understanding of the relationship between people and the land.

## Promoting Sustainability

Collaborating with others to forage responsibly and ethically helps protect wild ecosystems and ensure the long-term availability of wild foods for future generations. Sharing information about sustainable harvesting practices encourages the communities to prioritize conservation and stewardship when gathering wild plants and mushrooms, helping maintain the health and biodiversity of local ecosystems.

## Strengthening Resilience

Building a culture of sharing and collaboration in foraging strengthens the resilience of local communities by developing mutual support and cooperation. By working together to share resources, skills, and experiences, community members can better navigate challenges like food insecurity, environmental degradation, and climate change, ultimately building more resilient and sustainable communities.

As mentioned earlier, living a foraging lifestyle is more than just about finding food. Foraging is about finding meaning, purpose, and fulfillment in your relationship with the Earth and all its inhabitants. Beyond simply gathering food, foraging becomes a deeply enriching experience that nourishes not just your body but also your soul.

In the simplicity of gathering wild foods, you discover a profound connection to the natural world. Each plant, mushroom, and berry has a connection in the intricate network of life, reminding you of your connection with the Earth. Through foraging, you learn to listen to nature's rhythms, respect its cycles, and appreciate its abundance.

It's foraging that teaches you humility, reminding you of your place in the vast web of life. It helps you to be thankful for the gifts that nature provides, making you deeply respect the land and its resources.

Living a foraging lifestyle is a journey of self-discovery and personal growth. It challenges you to step outside of your comfort zone, embrace uncertainty, and trust in the wisdom of the natural world. It invites you to be mindful, present, and thankful in your daily life, giving you a deeper sense of purpose and satisfaction.

Ultimately, living a foraging lifestyle is a deeply transformative experience that nourishes your body and your spirit. It encourages you to rethink your relationship with the Earth and all its inhabitants, inspiring you to live more consciously, kindly, and in harmony.

# Bonus: Southwest Foraging Calendar

## Southwest Foraging Calendar

| | | | | Jan | Feb | Mar | Apr | May | Jun | Jul | Aug | Sep | Oct | Nov | Dec |
|---|---|---|---|---|---|---|---|---|---|---|---|---|---|---|---|
| ❄ Winter | 🌱 Spring | ☀ Summer | 🍁 Fall | | | | | | | | | | | | |
| 🌱 SPRING | | | | | | | | | | | | | | | |
| Desert Parsley | | | | | | 🌱 | | | | | | | | | |
| Desert Shaggy Mane | | | | | | 🌱 | | | | | | | | | |
| Desert Lily | | | | | | 🌱 | | | | | | | | | |
| Evening Primrose | | | | | | 🌱 | | | | | | | | | |
| Hedgehog Mushroom | | | | | | 🌱 | | | | | | | | | |
| Indian Paintbrush | | | | | | 🌱 | | | | | | | | | |
| Lamb's Quarters | | | | | | 🌱 | | | | | | | | | |
| Miner's Lettuce | | | | | | 🌱 | | | | | | | | | |
| Morchella species (Morels) | | | | | | 🌱 | | | | | | | | | |
| Nettles | | | | | | 🌱 | | | | | | | | | |
| Ocotillo (Fouquieria splendens) | | | | | | 🌱 | | | | | | | | | |
| Prickly Pear Cactus Flowers | | | | | | 🌱 | | | | | | | | | |
| Saguaro Cactus | | | | | | 🌱 | | | | | | | | | |
| Sego Lily Bulbs | | | | | | 🌱 | | | | | | | | | |
| Palo Verde (Parkinsonia spp.) | | | | | | 🌱 | | | | | | | | | |
| Tuberous Sow Thistle | | | | | | 🌱 | | | | | | | | | |
| Wild Onion | | | | | | 🌱 | | | | | | | | | |
| Wood Sorrel | | | | | | 🌱 | | | | | | | | | |
| Yucca Flowers | | | | | | 🌱 | | | | | | | | | |

| ❄ Winter 🌿 Spring ☀ Summer 🍂 Fall | Jan | Feb | Mar | Apr | May | Jun | Jul | Aug | Sep | Oct | Nov | Dec |
|---|---|---|---|---|---|---|---|---|---|---|---|---|
| **🌿 SPRING** | | | | | | | | | | | | |
| Chaparral (Larrea tridentata) | | | ■ | ■ | ■ | ■ | ■ | ■ | ■ | 🌿 | | |
| Wild Mint (Mentha arvensis) | | | | ■ | ■ | ■ | ■ | 🌿 | | | | |
| **☀ SUMMER** | | | | | | | | | | | | |
| Mullein (Verbascum thapsus) | | | | | ■ | ☀ | | | | | | |
| Agaricus species (Mushrooms) | | | | | ■ | ☀ | | | | | | |
| Amaranth Seeds | | | | | ■ | ☀ | | | | | | |
| Chickweed | | | | | ■ | ☀ | | | | | | |
| Elderberry | | | | | ■ | ☀ | | | | | | |
| Fishhook Cactus | | | | | ■ | ☀ | | | | | | |
| Indian Potato | | | | | ■ | ☀ | | | | | | |
| Jojoba Seeds | | | | | ■ | ☀ | | | | | | |
| Lamb's Quarters | | | | | ■ | ☀ | | | | | | |
| Lion's Mane (Mushroom) | | | | | ■ | ☀ | | | | | | |
| Mallow | | | | | ■ | ☀ | | | | | | |
| Mesquite Pods | | | | | ■ | ☀ | | | | | | |
| Wild Amaranth | | | | | ■ | ☀ | | | | | | |
| Wolfberry | | | | | ■ | ☀ | | | | | | |
| Amaranth Seeds | | | | | ■ | ☀ | | | | | | |
| Juniper (Juniperus spp.) | | | | | | ■ | ■ | ☀ | | | | |
| Arnica (Arnica spp.) | | | | | ■ | ☀ | | | | | | |

## ♣ FALL

| | Jan | Feb | Mar | Apr | May | Jun | Jul | Aug | Sep | Oct | Nov | Dec |
|---|---|---|---|---|---|---|---|---|---|---|---|---|
| Echinacea (Echinacea spp.) | | | | | | ▓ | ▓ | ▓ | | | | |
| Acorns | | | | | | | ▓ | ▓ | ▓ | | | |
| Agaricus species | | | | ▓ | ▓ | ▓ | ▓ | | | | | |
| Black Trumpet (Mushroom) | | | | | | | ▓ | ▓ | ▓ | | | |
| Chiltepín Seeds | | | | | | | ▓ | ▓ | ▓ | | | |
| Chokecherry | | | | | | | ▓ | ▓ | ▓ | | | |
| Desert Hackberry | | | | | | | ▓ | ▓ | ▓ | | | |
| Dandelion | | | | | | | ▓ | ▓ | ▓ | | | |
| King Bolete (Mushroom) | | | | | | | ▓ | ▓ | ▓ | | | |
| Mesquite Pods | | | | | | | ▓ | ▓ | ▓ | | | |
| Miner's Lettuce | | | | | | | ▓ | ▓ | ▓ | | | |
| Oyster Mushrooms | | | | | | | ▓ | ▓ | ▓ | | | |
| Pinyon Pine Nuts | | | | | | | ▓ | ▓ | ▓ | | | |
| Prickly Pear Cactus | | | | | | | ▓ | ▓ | ▓ | | | |
| Pumpkin Seeds | | | | | | | ▓ | ▓ | ▓ | | | |
| Sumac | | | | | | | ▓ | ▓ | ▓ | | | |
| Wild Amaranth | | | | | | | ▓ | ▓ | ▓ | | | |
| Wolfberry | | | | | | | ▓ | ▓ | ▓ | | | |

| | ❄ Winter | ☘ Spring | ☀ Summer | ♣ Fall | Jan | Feb | Mar | Apr | May | Jun | Jul | Aug | Sep | Oct | Nov | Dec |
|---|---|---|---|---|---|---|---|---|---|---|---|---|---|---|---|---|

## WINTER

| | Jan | Feb | Mar | Apr | May | Jun | Jul | Aug | Sep | Oct | Nov | Dec |
|---|---|---|---|---|---|---|---|---|---|---|---|---|
| Chickweed | ❄ | | | | | | | | | ❄ | | |
| Hedgehog Mushroom | ❄ | | | | | | | | | ❄ | | |
| Miner's Lettuce | ❄ | | | | | | | | | ❄ | | |
| Prickly Pear Cactus | ❄ | | | | | | | | | ❄ | | |
| Sunchoke | ❄ | | | | | | | | | ❄ | | |

# Index

# Toxic Plants and Fungi List for Wild Edibles

## Agaricus xanthodermus (Yellow-staining Mushroom)

- **Looks Like:** Edible Agaricus species (such as Agaricus campestris)
- **Differentiating Factor:** The yellow-staining Mushroom has a yellow discoloration at the base of the stem when cut or bruised, and the gills turn yellow when rubbed.
- **Toxic Compounds:** Phenol compounds
- **Effects:** Can cause gastrointestinal distress, including nausea, vomiting, and diarrhea.

## Barrel Cactus (Ferocactus spp.)

- **Looks Like:** Edible Barrel Cactus species (Ferocactus wislizeni)
- **Differentiating Factor:** Toxic Barrel Cactus species may have dense clusters of long, straight spines, while edible Barrel Cactus species often have fewer, hooked spines.
- **Toxic Compounds:** Hordenine and other alkaloids
- **Effects:** Can cause nausea and vomiting.
- **Chaparral (Larrea tridentata)**
- **Looks Like:** Creosote bush (similar in appearance to Chaparral)
- **Differentiating Factor:** Chaparral has small, resinous, olive-green leaves and yellow flowers.

**Toxic Compounds:** Nordihydroguaiaretic acid (NDGA)

- **Effects:** Can cause liver and kidney damage when ingested in large amounts.
- **Chokecherry (Prunus virginiana)**
- **Looks Like:** Edible berries such as Elderberry (Sambucus spp.)
- **Differentiating Factor:** Chokecherry has clusters of small, round, dark purple to black berries with a single stone and leaves with finely serrated edges.
- **Toxic Compounds:** Cyanogenic glycosides
- **Effects:** Releases cyanide when consumed, potentially leading to symptoms of cyanide poisoning, including headache, dizziness,

confusion, and, in severe cases, respiratory failure.

## Desert Lily (Hesperocallis undulata)

- **Looks Like:** Edible lily species
- **Differentiating Factor:** Desert Lily has large, white to cream-colored flowers with long, narrow petals and a basal rosette of strap-like leaves.
- **Toxic Compounds:** Toxic alkaloids
- **Effects:** Can cause gastrointestinal distress, including nausea and vomiting.
- **Desert Marigold (Baileya multiradiata)**
- **Looks Like:** Edible wildflowers
- **Differentiating Factor:** Desert Marigold has bright yellow, daisy-like flowers with finely divided, silvery-gray leaves.

**Toxic Compounds:** Sesquiterpene lactones

- **Effects:** Can cause gastrointestinal distress and dermatitis if ingested or handled.
- **Elderberry (Sambucus spp.)**
- **Looks Like:** Edible berries such as Blueberry (Vaccinium spp.)
- **Differentiating Factor:** Elderberry has compound leaves with 5 to 11 leaflets, white to cream-colored flat-topped flower clusters, and purple-black berries in dense clusters.
- **Toxic Compounds:** Cyanogenic glycosides
- **Effects:** Releases cyanide when consumed, potentially causing nausea, vomiting, diarrhea, and, in severe cases, cyanide poisoning.

## Indian Paintbrush (Castilleja spp.)

- **Looks Like:** Edible wildflowers
- **Differentiating Factor:** Indian Paintbrush has brightly colored bracts (red, orange, yellow) that surround the actual flower, giving it a brush-like appearance.
- **Toxic Compounds:** Alkaloids
- **Effects:** Can cause gastrointestinal distress and other symptoms if ingested.

### Jojoba Seeds (Simmondsia chinensis)

- **Looks Like:** Edible seeds and nuts
- **Differentiating Factor:** Jojoba plants have gray-green, oval leaves and small, greenish-yellow flowers. The seeds are smooth and oval-shaped.
- **Toxic Compounds:** Simmondsin
- **Effects:** Can cause nausea, vomiting, and other symptoms if ingested.

### Mullein (Verbascum thapsus)

- **Looks Like:** Edible leafy greens
- **Differentiating Factor:** Mullein has large, woolly, gray-green leaves and a tall spike of yellow flowers.
- **Toxic Compounds:** Saponins and rotenone
- **Effects:** Can cause gastrointestinal distress if ingested.

### Ocotillo (Fouquieria splendens)

- **Looks Like:** Edible cacti
- **Differentiating Factor:** Ocotillo has long, spiny stems that produce clusters of bright red flowers at the tips.
- **Toxic Compounds:** Alkaloids
- **Effects:** Can cause gastrointestinal distress and other symptoms if consumed.

### Prickly Pear Cactus (Opuntia spp.)

- **Looks Like:** Edible Prickly Pear species
- **Differentiating Factor:** While most Prickly Pear species are edible, some may contain toxic compounds like oxalates, which can cause gastrointestinal distress and kidney stones if consumed in large quantities.
- **Toxic Compounds:** Oxalates
- **Effects:** Can cause gastrointestinal distress and kidney stones if consumed in large quantities.

**Saguaro Cactus (Carnegiea gigantea)**

- **Looks Like:** Other edible cacti
- **Differentiating Factor:** Saguaro has tall, columnar stems with numerous ribs and white flowers that bloom at the tops of the stems.
- **Toxic Compounds:** Alkaloids
- **Effects:** It can be toxic if consumed, causing nausea and other symptoms.

**Wood Sorrel (Oxalis spp.)**

- **Looks Like:** Edible leafy greens
- **Differentiating Factor:** Wood Sorrel has heart-shaped leaflets that fold at night and produce small, five-petaled flowers that can be yellow, white, or pink.
- **Toxic Compounds:** Oxalic acid
- **Effects:** It can be toxic in large quantities and should be consumed in moderation to avoid kidney stones and other health issues.

**Note:** Always ensure positive identification and consult reliable foraging resources before consuming any wild plant or mushroom.

# Conclusion

You've read all the information about foraging, from discovering wild edibles in various terrains to tapping into the Southwestern foraging lifestyle.

In the first chapters, you learned the basics of foraging in the Southwest, understood essential equipment and safety measures, and discovered the region's seasonal rhythms. With this information, exploring any landscape and foraging wild edibles in the Southwest won't be a problem.

You've read about various wild edible plants that thrive in the arid climate, from the familiar prickly pear cactus to the lesser-known desert sage. You've expanded your culinary knowledge by uncovering wild mushrooms in the region and learning to identify safe and delicious species to add to your meals.

With a collection of mouthwatering recipes, you've explored how to cook with wild edibles, transforming your foraged finds into dishes that celebrate the flavors of the Southwest. From salads to soups, main courses to desserts, you name it – each recipe takes you back in time.

However, your journey doesn't end with food. You've also read about medicinal plants, discovered the healing properties of native herbs and flowers, and learned how to harness their power for health and wellness.

Throughout the chapters, you have been encouraged to follow the principles of sustainability and respect, understanding the importance of preserving these delicate ecosystems for future generations. Not following sustainable and ethical practices in foraging will only disrupt the habitat and potentially endanger the ecosystem.-

While you have read everything required for foraging in the Southwest, it's time to start planning your adventure. However, please keep in mind that you will need practice with certain skills, such as using foraging tools safely, navigating different terrains, and, most importantly, properly identifying the wild edibles that are safe to consume.

If you enjoyed this book, I'd greatly appreciate a review on Amazon because it helps me to create more books that people want. It would mean a lot to hear from you.

**To leave a review:**
1. Open your camera app.
2. Point your mobile device at the QR code.
3. The review page will appear in your web browser.

*Thanks for your support!*

# Here's another book by Dion Rosser that you might like

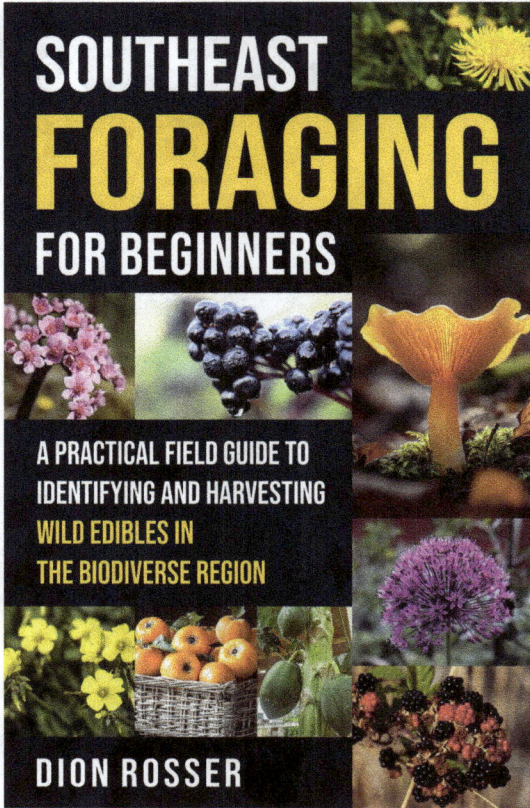

# References

Kubala, J. (2021, June 3). Foraging for Food: Tips, Common Foods, Safety, and More. Healthline. https://www.healthline.com/nutrition/foraging-for-food

Mihail, A. (2023, July 11). Foraging in The Modern World: Rediscovering an Ancient Practice. Www.foodunfolded.com. https://www.foodunfolded.com/article/foraging-in-the-modern-world-rediscovering-an-ancient-practice

Southwest. (n.d.). Www.swcs.org. https://www.swcs.org/about-us/our-chapters/southwest

Young, D. (2023, April 6). Ethical Foraging 101: What You Need to Know. LearningHerbs. https://learningherbs.com/blog/foraging/

Blankespoor, J., & Gemma, M. (2019, March 8). Essential Foraging Tools and Supplies. Chestnut School of Herbal Medicine. https://chestnutherbs.com/essential-foraging-tools-and-supplies/

Borke, J. (2023, November 2). Jimsonweed poisoning: MedlinePlus Medical Encyclopedia. Medlineplus.gov. https://medlineplus.gov/ency/article/002881.htm

Fertig, W. (n.d.). Water Hemlock. Www.fs.usda.gov. https://www.fs.usda.gov/wildflowers/plant-of-the-week/cicuta_maculata.shtml

Forager, J. (2018, January 4). Foraging Fatality Statistics 2016 (Please Share). Eat the Planet. https://eattheplanet.org/foraging-fatality-statistics-2016/

Frank, A. von. (2018, May 3). Why You Should Leave the Roots from Your Old Garden Plants in the Ground. GrowJourney. https://www.growjourney.com/why-you-should-leave-the-roots-from-your-old-garden-plants-in-the-ground/

Hazzard, C. (2015, April 1). Hiking Boots or Shoes: Do I Really Need Hiking Boots? HikingGuy.com. https://hikingguy.com/how-to-hike/hiking-boots-or-shoes-do-i-really-need-hiking-boots/

Krochmal, C. (2017, April 24). Southwest Foraging | Bee Culture. Bee Culture. https://www.beeculture.com/southwest-foraging/

Mayo Clinic. (2018). Poison Ivy Rash - Symptoms and Causes. Mayo Clinic. https://www.mayoclinic.org/diseases-conditions/poison-ivy/symptoms-causes/syc-20376485

McDonald, C. (n.d.). Mountain Deathcamas. Www.fs.usda.gov. https://www.fs.usda.gov/wildflowers/plant-of-the-week/zigadenus_elegans.shtml

US Department of Commerce, N. (n.d.). It Does Get Cold in Northern Arizona. Www.weather.gov. https://www.weather.gov/fgz/Cold

Zabel, H. H. (2022, July 1). Climate of the Southwestern United States. Earth@Home. https://earthathome.org/hoe/sw/climate/

Gauger, E. (n.d.). Desert Southwest (Explore America's Southwestern Deserts). Notes from the Road. https://www.notesfromtheroad.com/desertsouthwest/

Krochmal, C. (2017, April 24). Southwest Foraging | Bee Culture. Bee Culture. https://www.beeculture.com/southwest-foraging/

Southwest USA Landscapes - Deserts. (n.d.). Www.americansouthwest.net. https://www.americansouthwest.net/deserts.html

What to Forage & Wildcraft in Each Season. (2022, January 15). Gather & Grow. https://gatherandgrow.com/blog/what-to-forage-amp-wildcraft-in-each-season

Blizzard, K. (2017, May 1). Wild Edible Plants and Weeds in Colorado - Spring Foraging with the Wild Food Girl. Modern Forager. https://modern-forager.com/wild-edible-plants-in-colorado/

Leikam, E. (2020, August 20). Nature Provides: Edible Wild Plants You Can Forage in the USA. Www.kuhl.com. https://www.kuhl.com/borninthemountains/edible-plants-on-the-trails-in-usa

Partners, S. B. (2020, May 21). Edible Flowers. Savor the Southwest: https://savorthesouthwest.blog/tag/edible-flowers/

Southwest Foraging | Bee Culture. (2017, April 24). https://www.beeculture.com/southwest-foraging/

Southwest Foraging Guide. (n.d.). FarmSteady. https://farmsteady.com/products/southwest-foraging-guide-book

Winter Mushroom Foraging In The Southwest - Mushroom Appreciation. (2023, December 20). Www.mushroom-Appreciation.com. https://www.mushroom-appreciation.com/winter-mushroom-foraging-in-the-southwest.html

Blizzard, K. (2018, July 18). 5 Colorado High Elevation Wild Mushrooms. Modern Forager. https://modern-forager.com/colorado-wild-edible-mushrooms/

Foraging — Swampy Appleseed Mushrooms. (n.d.). Swampy Appleseed Mushrooms. https://www.swampyappleseed.com/foraging

Glossary of Useful Terms. (n.d.). Fungimap. https://fungimap.org.au/about-fungi/glossary-of-useful-terms/

Jesse. (2021, February 4). Mushroom Foraging Seasons of the Southeast - Feral Foraging. Feral Foraging. https://feralforaging.com/mushroom-foraging-seasons-of-the-southeast/

Mushroom Foraging Safety. (n.d.). Cascade Mycological Society. https://cascademyco.org/mushroom-info-menu-guide/mushroom-foraging-safety/

Acorn Squash Soup & Toasted Seeds Recipe by Hi, it's me! (2019, November 5). Cookpad. https://cookpad.com/us/recipes/10969812-acorn-squash-soup-toasted-seeds

Bergo, A. (2016, August 26). Classic Fried Puffballs. Forager | Chef. https://foragerchef.com/classic-fried-puffballs/#recipe

Beth. (2012, February 19). Hearty Black Bean Quesadillas - Vegetarian - with VIDEO. Budget Bytes. https://www.budgetbytes.com/hearty-black-bean-quesadillas/

Chavez, S. (2015, February 5). Green Chile Enchilada Recipe Made With Mushrooms and Nopalitos. Www.latinofoodie.com. https://www.latinofoodie.com/featured-blog-posts/greenenchiladas-with-nopalitos-and-mushrooms/

Denny, K. (2016, July 25). Purslane Salad with Lettuce, Tomatoes, Cucumbers, and Mint. Kalyn's Kitchen. https://kalynskitchen.com/mediterranean-lettuce-salad-recipe-with/#mv-creation-664-jtr

Donofrio, J. (2022, October 20). Acorn Squash Soup. Love and Lemons. https://www.loveandlemons.com/acorn-squash-soup/#wprm-recipe-container-66136

Gravalese, S. (2024, May 2). 10 Tips for Cooking with Wild Edibles. Slow Living Kitchen. https://slowlivingkitchen.com/cooking-with-wild-edibles/

Indian Paintbrush Fruit Salad. (n.d.). Www.dvo.com. https://www.dvo.com/recipe_pages/mountainwest/Indian_Paintbrush_Fruit_Salad.php

Jackson, L. (2023, April 29). Wild Onion Pasta | cookeatworld.com. Cook Eat World. https://www.cookeatworld.com/wild-onion-pasta/

Jennifer. (2019, June 25). Crema Recipe. Carlsbad Cravings. https://carlsbadcravings.com/avocado-crema/#wprm-recipe-container-34424

johnsoulesfoods. (2022, September 2). Cooking Tips for Beginners. JohnSoulesFoods. https://www.johnsoulesfoods.com/blog/cooking-tips-for-beginners/

Kalin. (2020, June 25). Mexican Sauteed Vegetables. Abundance of Flavor. https://www.abundanceofflavor.com/mexican-sauteed-vegetables/#google_vignette

Krista. (2019, September 8). Sheet Pan Veggie Tacos with Avocado Lime Crema - Destination Delish. Destination Delish. https://www.destinationdelish.com/sheet-pan-veggie-tacos-with-avocado-lime-crema/

MARIGOLD PETALS. (n.d.). David Vanille. https://www.davidvanille.com/en/spices-and-seasonning/531-marigold-petals.html

Martínez, M. (2009, June 26). How To Cook Nopales (Cactus Paddles) | Quick and Easy! Mexico in My Kitchen. https://www.mexicoinmykitchen.com/how-to-cook-cactus-paddles/#recipe

Matsoukas, G. (2022, May 23). Garlic Mashed Yuca Root (Mashed Cassava). Running to the Kitchen®. https://www.runningtothekitchen.com/garlic-mashed-yuca/#wprm-recipe-container-33979

Melancon, N. (2023, July 22). Nopales (prickly pear cactus) tacos. Www.bbc.com. https://www.bbc.com/travel/article/20230721-prickly-pear-cactus-tacos

Meme. (2021, March 23). Wolfberry Leaves & Seeds Soup Recipe by Meme. Cookpad. https://cookpad.com/us/recipes/14772860-wolfberry-leaves-seeds-soup

Miller-Ka, N. (2018, November 29). Southern Savory Onion Pie. Nik Snacks. https://www.niksnacksonline.com/2018/11/savory-onion-pie.html

Morel Mushroom Pizza With Sausage & Green Garlic. (2020, May 11). Dishing up the Dirt. https://dishingupthedirt.com/recipes/morel-mushroom-pizza-green-garlic-sausage/

Saima. (2019, May 26). Potato Curry with Poori (Aloo Poori). Indian Ambrosia. https://indianambrosia.com/aloo-curry/

Sterner, H. (2021, August 29). Wild Huckleberry Jam. Hilda's Kitchen Blog. https://hildaskitchenblog.com/recipe/wild-huckleberry-jam-recipe/#recipe

Stuffed Peppers with Wild Rice and Mushrooms. (n.d.). Idaho Preferred. https://idahopreferred.com/recipes/stuffed-peppers-with-wild-rice-and-mushrooms/

Weaver, S. (2011, October 10). Prickly Pear Cactus Fruit Sorbet. Migraine Relief Recipes. https://migrainereliefrecipes.com/prickly-pear-cactus-fruit-sorbet/

Chaparral. (2022, August 16). Www.cancerresearchuk.org. https://www.cancerresearchuk.org/about-cancer/treatment/complementary-alternative-therapies/individual-therapies/chaparral

Chen, S.-L., Yu, H., Luo, H.-M., Wu, Q., Li, C.-F., & Steinmetz, A. (2016). Conservation and Sustainable Use of Medicinal Plants: Problems, Progress, and Prospects. Chinese Medicine, 11(1). https://doi.org/10.1186/s13020-016-0108-7

Guzman, I. (n.d.). Medicinal Plants. https://desertblooms.nmsu.edu/documents/ready-set-grow-07_21_2021-ivette-guzman-medicinal-plants.pdf

Mathura, K. (2021). Southwest Native Herbs. https://www.chandleraz.gov/sites/default/files/Southwest-Native-Herbs-QC.pdf

Medicinal Botany. (n.d.). Www.fs.usda.gov. https://www.fs.usda.gov/wildflowers/ethnobotany/medicinal/index.shtml

Min, F. N. 5. (2020, May 29). Top 5 Medicinal Plants of the Southwest. The Filson Journal. https://www.filson.com/blog/field-notes/top-5-medicinal-plants-of-the-southwest/

Petrovska, B. B. (2012). Historical Review of Medicinal Plants' Usage. Pharmacognosy Reviews, 6(11), 1. https://doi.org/10.4103/0973-7847.95849

Saville, D. (2016). Herbalism in the Crossroads of the Southwest | Albuquerque Herbalism. Albuquerqueherbalism.com. https://albuquerqueherbalism.com/2016/01/10/herbalism-in-the-crossroads-of-the-southwest/

Foraging for the Future: Incorporating Wild Edibles into Your Emergency. (2023, April 4). Food Bunker. https://foodbunker.co.uk/blogs/food-preparation-storage/foraging-for-the-future-incorporating-wild-edibles-into-your-uk-emergency-food-supply

Reciprocal Foraging. (n.d.). Wild Pigment Project. https://wildpigmentproject.org/reciprocal-foraging

Roy, N. (2023, August 7). 5 Lesser-Known Traditional Ways of Preserving Food for a Long Time. The Times of India. https://timesofindia.indiatimes.com/life-style/food-news/5-lesser-known-traditional-ways-of-preserving-food-for-a-long-time/photostory/102504310.cms

Thomas, C. (2022, April 21). Fermentation for Long-Term Preservation. Homesteading Family. https://homesteadingfamily.com/fermentation-for-long-term-preservation/

Tippins, N. (2016, January 20). Wild Food for Busy People: Easy Ways To Include Wild Food In Your Diet. Wild Heart Food. https://wildheartfood.com/wild-food-diet-for-busy-people/

# Image Sources

[1] *https://www.pexels.com/photo/green-leafed-tree-38136/*

[2] *James Case from Philadelphia, Mississippi, U.S.A., CC BY 2.0 <https://creativecommons.org/licenses/by/2.0>, via Wikimedia Commons. https://commons.wikimedia.org/wiki/File:Victorinox_Pruning_Knife_(8754348826).jpg*

[3] *Mbotke, CC BY 3.0 <https://creativecommons.org/licenses/by/3.0>, via Wikimedia Commons. https://commons.wikimedia.org/wiki/File:Mojave_Desert_morning_CA_2005.JPG*

[4] *Miguel Angel Omaña Rojas, CC0, via Wikimedia Commons. https://commons.wikimedia.org/wiki/File:Nopal_Cactus_with_flower.jpg*

[5] *barockschloss from Zeilitzheim, Germany, CC BY 2.0 <https://creativecommons.org/licenses/by/2.0>, via Wikimedia Commons. https://commons.wikimedia.org/wiki/File:Pruning_shears.jpg*

[6] *James St. John, CC BY 2.0 <https://creativecommons.org/licenses/by/2.0>, via Wikimedia Commons. https://commons.wikimedia.org/wiki/File:Toxicodendron_radicans_(poison_ivy)_2_(49046043216).jpg*

[7] *Justin Meissen from St Paul, United States, CC BY-SA 2.0 <https://creativecommons.org/licenses/by-sa/2.0>, via Wikimedia Commons. https://commons.wikimedia.org/wiki/File:Jimsonweed_(13496651184).jpg*

[8] *Water dropwort hemlock, Drumardnagross by Kenneth Allen, CC BY-SA 2.0 <https://creativecommons.org/licenses/by-sa/2.0>, via Wikimedia Commons. https://commons.wikimedia.org/wiki/File:Water_dropwort_hemlock,_Drumardnagross_-_geograph.org.uk_-_6221963.jpg*

[9] *Bureau of Land Management Oregon and Washington, Public domain, via Wikimedia Commons. https://commons.wikimedia.org/wiki/File:Death_camas_Zygadenus_venenosus_2_(17842490404).jpg*

[10] *https://commons.wikimedia.org/wiki/File:Sweet_cherries_in_basket_2018_G1.jpg*

[11] shrinkin'violet from Bristol, UK, CC BY 2.0 <https://creativecommons.org/licenses/by/2.0>, via Wikimedia Commons. https://commons.wikimedia.org/wiki/File:My_trusty_gardening_gloves_%26_secateurs_which_need_a_good_clean_by_the_look_of_them_(8711272274).jpg

[12] CDC, Public domain, via Wikimedia Commons. https://commons.wikimedia.org/wiki/File:A-first-aid-kit.jpg

[13] Dick Culbert, CC BY 2.0 <https://creativecommons.org/licenses/by/2.0>, via Wikimedia Commons. https://commons.wikimedia.org/wiki/File:007_prickly_pear.jpg

[14] Ricraider, CC BY-SA 3.0 <https://creativecommons.org/licenses/by-sa/3.0>, via Wikimedia Commons. https://commons.wikimedia.org/wiki/File:Chihuahuan_Desert.jpg

[15] Chris Light, CC BY-SA 4.0 <https://creativecommons.org/licenses/by-sa/4.0>, via Wikimedia Commons. https://commons.wikimedia.org/wiki/File:Wild_Grape_8078.jpg

[16] Photo by David J. Stang, CC BY-SA 4.0 <https://creativecommons.org/licenses/by-sa/4.0>, via Wikimedia Commons. https://commons.wikimedia.org/wiki/File:Salvia_officinalis_Berggarten_2zz.jpg

[17] James St. John, CC BY 2.0 <https://creativecommons.org/licenses/by/2.0>, via Wikimedia Commons. https://commons.wikimedia.org/wiki/File:Opuntia_phaeacantha_(desert_prickly_pear_cactus)_(No_Thoroughfare_Canyon,_Colorado_National_Monument,_Colorado,_USA)_9_(23954245035).jpg

[18] Gillfoto, CC BY-SA 4.0 <https://creativecommons.org/licenses/by-sa/4.0>, via Wikimedia Commons. https://commons.wikimedia.org/wiki/File:Fishhook_Barrel_Cactus_894.jpg

[19] Stan Shebs, CC BY-SA 3.0 <https://creativecommons.org/licenses/by-sa/3.0>, via Wikimedia Commons https://commons.wikimedia.org/wiki/File:Cylindropuntia_acanthocarpa_var_coloradensis_4.jpg

[20] WClarke, CC BY-SA 3.0 <https://creativecommons.org/licenses/by-sa/3.0>, via Wikimedia Commons https://commons.wikimedia.org/wiki/File:Carnegiea_gigantea_in_Saguaro_National_Park_near_Tucson%2C_Arizona_during_November_%2858%29.jpg

[21] https://commons.wikimedia.org/wiki/File:Fishhook_cactus_(1).jpg

[22] The original uploader was Pretzelpaws at English Wikipedia., CC BY-SA 3.0 <http://creativecommons.org/licenses/by-sa/3.0/>, via Wikimedia Commons. https://commons.wikimedia.org/wiki/File:Organ_pipe_cactus.jpg

[23] Peter Burka, CC BY-SA 2.0 <https://creativecommons.org/licenses/by-sa/2.0>, via Wikimedia Commons. https://commons.wikimedia.org/wiki/File:Lamb%27s_quarters_(51301524882).jpg

[24] Muséum de Toulouse, CC BY-SA 4.0 <https://creativecommons.org/licenses/by-sa/4.0>, via Wikimedia Commons. https://commons.wikimedia.org/wiki/File:Portulaca_oleracea_MHNT.jpg

[25] Robert Flogaus-Faust, CC BY 4.0 <https://creativecommons.org/licenses/by/4.0>, via Wikimedia Commons. https://commons.wikimedia.org/wiki/File:Claytonia_perfoliata_2_RF.jpg

[26] Pompilid, CC BY-SA 3.0 <http://creativecommons.org/licenses/by-sa/3.0/>, via Wikimedia Commons https://commons.wikimedia.org/wiki/File:Amaranthus_palmeri.jpg

[27] W. Carter, CC0, via Wikimedia Commons. https://commons.wikimedia.org/wiki/File:Nettles_in_R%C3%B6e_g%C3%A5rd_4.jpg

[28] Markus Bernet, CC BY-SA 2.0 <https://creativecommons.org/licenses/by-sa/2.0>, via Wikimedia Commons. https://commons.wikimedia.org/wiki/File:Dandelion_clock.jpg

[29] W. Carter, CC0, via Wikimedia Commons. https://commons.wikimedia.org/wiki/File:Wood_sorrel_after_rain.jpg

[30] Michel Langeveld, CC BY-SA 4.0 <https://creativecommons.org/licenses/by-sa/4.0>, via Wikimedia Commons. https://commons.wikimedia.org/wiki/File:Stellaria_media_171768008.jpg

[31] Robert Flogaus-Faust, CC BY 4.0 <https://creativecommons.org/licenses/by/4.0>, via Wikimedia Commons. https://commons.wikimedia.org/wiki/File:Malva_sylvestris_3_RF.jpg

[32] Leslie Seaton from Seattle, WA, USA, CC BY 2.0 <https://creativecommons.org/licenses/by/2.0>, via Wikimedia Commons. https://commons.wikimedia.org/wiki/File:Desert_Marigold_(5300809639).jpg

[33] https://commons.wikimedia.org/wiki/File:Prickly_pear_cactus_orange_flowers_opuntia_humifusa.jpg

[34] Axdae, CC BY-SA 4.0 <https://creativecommons.org/licenses/by-sa/4.0>, via Wikimedia Commons. https://commons.wikimedia.org/wiki/File:Yucca_flowers_(281110098).jpg

[35] Velvetlady0, CC BY-SA 4.0 <https://creativecommons.org/licenses/by-sa/4.0>, via Wikimedia Commons. https://commons.wikimedia.org/wiki/File:Saguaro_Cactus_Bloom.jpg

[36] Katja Schulz from Washington, D. C., USA, CC BY 2.0 <https://creativecommons.org/licenses/by/2.0>, via Wikimedia Commons. https://commons.wikimedia.org/wiki/File:Desert_Hackberry_-_Flickr_-_treegrow_(1).jpg

[37] Sten Porse, CC BY-SA 3.0 <http://creativecommons.org/licenses/by-sa/3.0/>, via Wikimedia Commons. https://commons.wikimedia.org/wiki/File:Lycium-barbarum-fruits.JPG

[38] https://commons.wikimedia.org/wiki/File:Prunus_virginiana_(chokecherry)_BLM.jpg

[39] ama, CC0, via Wikimedia Commons. https://commons.wikimedia.org/wiki/File:Sambucus_1.jpg

[40] Oneconscious at English Wikipedia, CC BY-SA 3.0 <https://creativecommons.org/licenses/by-sa/3.0>, via Wikimedia Commons. https://commons.wikimedia.org/wiki/File:SumacFruit.JPG

[41] Don A.W. Carlson, CC BY-SA 3.0 <http://creativecommons.org/licenses/by-sa/3.0/>, via Wikimedia Commons https://commons.wikimedia.org/wiki/File:Prosopis-glandulosa-seed-pods.jpg

[42] Dcrjsr, CC BY 3.0 <https://creativecommons.org/licenses/by/3.0>, via Wikimedia Commons. https://commons.wikimedia.org/wiki/File:Pinyon_cones_with_pine_nuts_-_Swall_Meadows,_Mono_County,_California.jpg

[43] Kenraiz, CC BY-SA 4.0 <https://creativecommons.org/licenses/by-sa/4.0>, via Wikimedia Commons https://commons.wikimedia.org/wiki/File:Quercus_gambelii_kz07.jpg

[44] Kenneth Bosma, CC BY 2.0 <https://creativecommons.org/licenses/by/2.0>, via Wikimedia Commons. https://commons.wikimedia.org/wiki/File:Jojoba.jpg

[45] https://commons.wikimedia.org/wiki/File:Salvia_columbariae.jpg

[46] *Trikutdas, CC BY-SA 4.0 <https://creativecommons.org/licenses/by-sa/4.0>, via Wikimedia Commons. https://commons.wikimedia.org/wiki/File:Potato_Plant-2.jpg*

[47] *Sokoloff PC, Murray DA, McBeth SR.M, Irvine MG, Rupert SM (2020) Additions to the "Martian Flora": new botanical records from the Mars Desert Research Station, Utah. Biodiversity Data Journal 8: e55063. https://doi.org/10.3897/BDJ.8.e55063, CC BY 4.0 <https://creativecommons.org/licenses/by/4.0>, via Wikimedia Commons https://commons.wikimedia.org/wiki/File:Allium_macropetalum_%2810.3897-BDJ.8.e55063%29_Figure_4_c.jpeg*

[48] *Dalgial, CC BY 3.0 <https://creativecommons.org/licenses/by/3.0>, via Wikimedia Commons https://commons.wikimedia.org/wiki/File:Helianthus_tuberosus_2.JPG*

[49] *https://commons.wikimedia.org/wiki/File:Fernleaf_Desert_Parsley_(339ba1396df245b888a 1fecb35f292b7).JPG*

[50] *Jim Morefield from Nevada, USA, CC BY-SA 2.0 <https://creativecommons.org/licenses/by-sa/2.0>, via Wikimedia Commons. https://commons.wikimedia.org/wiki/File:Desert_lily,_Hesperocallis_undulata_(15052841943).jpg*

[51] *https://commons.wikimedia.org/wiki/File:Plants_OB_686_(388508582222).jpg*

[52] *George Chernilevsky, CC BY-SA 4.0 <https://creativecommons.org/licenses/by-sa/4.0>, via Wikimedia Commons https://commons.wikimedia.org/wiki/File:Edible_mushrooms_in_baskets_2022_G1.jpg*

[53] *Agnes Monkelbaan, CC BY-SA 4.0 <https://creativecommons.org/licenses/by-sa/4.0>, via Wikimedia Commons. https://commons.wikimedia.org/wiki/File:Geschubde_inktzwam_ (Coprinus_comatus)._Locatie,_Paddenstoelenreservaat._11-10-2021._(actm.)_02.jpg*

[54] *James Lindsey at Ecology of Commanster, CC BY-SA 2.5 <https://creativecommons.org/licenses/by-sa/2.5>, via Wikimedia Commons. https://commons.wikimedia.org/wiki/File:Agaricus_spec._Lindsey_6.jpg*

[55] *Jerzy Opioła, CC BY-SA 4.0 <https://creativecommons.org/licenses/by-sa/4.0>, via Wikimedia Commons. https://commons.wikimedia.org/wiki/File:Laccaria_laccata_DK76.jpg*

[56] *Puffballs by Anne Burgess, CC BY-SA 2.0 <https://creativecommons.org/licenses/by-sa/2.0>, via Wikimedia Commons. https://commons.wikimedia.org/wiki/File:Puffballs_-_geograph.org.uk_-_3637726.jpg*

[57] *This image was created by user BlueCanoe at Mushroom Observer, CC BY-SA 3.0 <https://creativecommons.org/licenses/by-sa/3.0>, via Wikimedia Commons. https://commons.wikimedia.org/wiki/File:Morchella_brunnea_M.Kuo_222692.jpg*

[58] *Japonica, CC BY-SA 4.0 <https://creativecommons.org/licenses/by-sa/4.0>, via Wikimedia Commons. https://commons.wikimedia.org/wiki/File:Cantharellus_cibarius_-hym%C3%A9nium_fausses_lamelles.jpg*

[59] *Jack-o'-lantern mushroom by Richard Croft, CC BY-SA 2.0 <https://creativecommons.org/licenses/by-sa/2.0>, via Wikimedia Commons. https://commons.wikimedia.org/wiki/File:Jack-o%27-lantern_mushroom_-_geograph.org.uk_-_3748838.jpg*

[60] *Chiring Chandan, CC BY-SA 4.0 <https://creativecommons.org/licenses/by-sa/4.0>, via Wikimedia Commons.*
*https://commons.wikimedia.org/wiki/File:Pleurotus_ostreatus_(Oyster_Mushroom)_1.jpg*

[61] *Bernard Spragg. NZ from Christchurch, New Zealand, CC0, via Wikimedia Commons.*
*https://commons.wikimedia.org/wiki/File:King_Bolete._(36049252223).jpg*

[62] *Björn S..., CC BY-SA 2.0 <https://creativecommons.org/licenses/by-sa/2.0>, via Wikimedia Commons. https://commons.wikimedia.org/wiki/File:Tylopilus_felleus_(36878337253)_(2).jpg*

[63] *voir ci-dessous / see below, CC BY-SA 3.0 <https://creativecommons.org/licenses/by-sa/3.0>, via Wikimedia Commons.*
*https://commons.wikimedia.org/wiki/File:Laetiporus_sulphureus_JPG01.jpg*

[64] *Marko Vainu, CC BY-SA 3.0 <https://creativecommons.org/licenses/by-sa/3.0>, via Wikimedia Commons. https://commons.wikimedia.org/wiki/File:Craterellus_cornucopioides_Eestis.JPG*

[65] *gailhampshire, CC BY 2.0 <https://creativecommons.org/licenses/by/2.0>, via Wikimedia Commons. https://commons.wikimedia.org/wiki/File:Lion%27s_Mane_Fungi._Hericium_erinaceus.jpg*

[66] *Holger Krisp, CC BY 3.0 <https://creativecommons.org/licenses/by/3.0>, via Wikimedia Commons. https://commons.wikimedia.org/wiki/File:Semmel-Stoppelpilz_Semmelgelber_Stacheling_Hydnum_repandum.JPG*

[67] *https://www.pexels.com/photo/vegetable-salad-3026808/*

[68] *https://www.pexels.com/photo/lots-of-sliced-champignon-mushrooms-5848429/*

[69] *https://commons.wikimedia.org/wiki/File:Prosopis_velutina_seeds.jpg#/media/File:Prosopis_velutina_seeds.jpg*

[70] *Zeynel Cebeci, CC BY-SA 4.0 <https://creativecommons.org/licenses/by-sa/4.0>, via Wikimedia Commons. https://commons.wikimedia.org/wiki/File:Hint_inciri_-_Indian_fig_-_Opuntia_ficus-indica_02.JPG*

[71] *https://www.pexels.com/photo/vegetable-salad-on-white-plate-2862154/*

[72] *https://www.pexels.com/photo/cheese-pizza-2762942/*

[73] *Sonia Goyal Jaipur, CC BY-SA 2.0 <https://creativecommons.org/licenses/by-sa/2.0>, via Wikimedia Commons. https://commons.wikimedia.org/wiki/File:Yogurt_Potato_Curry_Recipe_From_North_Indian_Cuisine_By_Sonia_Goyal.jpg*

[74] *hobvias sudoneighm from Seattle, United States of America, CC BY 2.0 <https://creativecommons.org/licenses/by/2.0>, via Wikimedia Commons. https://commons.wikimedia.org/wiki/File:Trin%27s_onions_(772121262).jpg*

[75] *https://www.pexels.com/photo/three-round-pies-288264/*

[76] *https://www.pexels.com/photo/purple-petaled-flowers-in-mortar-and-pestle-105028/*

[77] *Krzysztof Ziarnek, Kenraiz, CC BY-SA 4.0 <https://creativecommons.org/licenses/by-sa/4.0>, via Wikimedia Commons. https://commons.wikimedia.org/wiki/File:Larrea_tridentata_kz03.jpg*

[78] *Shakeelgilgity, CC BY-SA 4.0 <https://creativecommons.org/licenses/by-sa/4.0>, via Wikimedia Commons. https://commons.wikimedia.org/wiki/File:Juniper_tree_of_Yasin.jpg*

[79] *Klearchos Kapoutsis from Santorini, Greece, CC BY 2.0 <https://creativecommons.org/licenses/by/2.0>, via Wikimedia Commons. https://commons.wikimedia.org/wiki/File:Saffron_gathering_(5214262838).jpg*

[80] *https://www.pexels.com/photo/photography-of-woman-using-laptop-1181681/*

[81] *Originally uploaded by Latch (Transferred by Szymon Żywicki), CC BY-SA 3.0 <https://creativecommons.org/licenses/by-sa/3.0>, via Wikimedia Commons. https://commons.wikimedia.org/wiki/File:Tomato_in_food_dehydrator.jpg*

www.ingramcontent.com/pod-product-compliance
Lightning Source LLC
Chambersburg PA
CBHW071942260326
41914CB00004B/719